SPOTLIGHT

D0814934

JACKSON HOLE, WYOMING

DON PITCHER

Contents

JACKSON HOLE

JACKSON HOLE

One of the most-visited slices of wild country in North America, Jackson Hole attracts well over three million travelers each year. They come here for a multitude of reasons: to camp under the stars in Grand Teton National Park, to play and shop in the New West town of Jackson, to hike flower-bedecked trails up forested valleys, to ride sleighs among thousands of elk, to raft down the Snake River, to ski or snowboard at one of three local resorts, or to simply stand in wonderment as the sun colors the sky behind the mountains. Many continue north to Yellowstone National Park, another place on everyone's must-see list. Drive north from Jackson toward Yellowstone and you'll quickly discover the biggest reason so many people are attracted to this place—its beauty. The Tetons act as a magnet, drawing your eyes away from the road and forcing you to stop and absorb some of their majesty. Welcome to one of the world's great wonderlands.

In the lingo of the mountain men, a "hole" was a large valley ringed by mountain ranges, and each was named for the trapper who based himself there. Jackson Hole, on Wyoming's far western border, is justifiably the most famous of all these intermountain valleys. Although Jackson Hole reaches an impressive 50 miles north to south and up to 16 miles across, the magnificent range of mountains to the west is what defines this valley. Shoshone Indians who wandered through this country called the peaks Teewinot (Many Pinnacles); later explorers would use such labels as Shark's Teeth or Pilot Knobs. But lonely French-Canadian trappers arriving in the early 1800s provided the

HIGHLIGHTS

◖ Visitor Center: Officially called the Jackson Hole & Greater Yellowstone Visitor Center, this large facility provides a one-stop introduction to the region, with information on the town, national forests, and the Elk Refuge (page 12).

◖ Town Square: Where else could you mix three million tourists, hundreds of elk antlers arranged in arches, and a faux shoot-out on summer evenings (page 12)?

◖ National Museum of Wildlife Art: One of Wyoming's top museums, with works by all the American masters, from Alfred Jacob Miller to Robert Bateman (page 14).

◖ National Elk Refuge: Winter is the peak season, with thousands of elk and horse-drawn sleighs in a scene straight out of Currier and Ives (page 16).

◖ River Rafting: Running the Snake River is a major summertime attraction, with many companies providing the raft and guide for a whitewater rock-and-roll or a gentle float trip past the Tetons (page 20).

◖ Jackson Hole Mountain Resort: This famous ski area keeps on trucking with all sorts of winter and summer activities – including an all-summer classical music festival, pop-jet fountains, and the tram up Rendezvous Mountain (page 31).

◖ Alaska Basin: This one's for backpackers, with access from Driggs, Idaho to the heart of the Teton Range. It's a gorgeous alpine valley, where high trails lead into Grand Teton National Park (page 79).

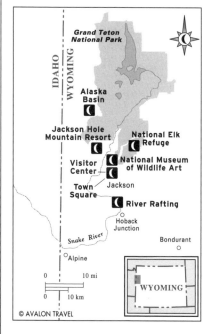

© AVALON TRAVEL

LOOK FOR ◖ TO FIND RECOMMENDED SIGHTS, ACTIVITIES, DINING, AND LODGING.

---

name that stuck: les Trois Tetons (literally, the Three Breasts).

The valley—originally called Jackson's Hole—was named for likable trapper David E. Jackson, one of the men who helped establish the Rocky Mountain Fur Company. When Jackson and his partners sold out in 1830, they realized a profit of more than $50,000. Jackson's presence remains in the names of both Jackson Hole and Jackson Lake. Eventually, more polite folks began calling the valley Jackson Hole in an attempt to end the ribald stories associated

with the name Jackson's Hole. (It's easy to imagine the jokes, with both Jackson's Hole and the Tetons in the same place.) In 1991, a group calling itself the Committee to Restore Decency to Our National Parks created quite a stir by suggesting that Grand Teton National Park be renamed. A letter sent to the Park Service and various members of Congress noted: "Though a great many Americans may be oblivious to this vulgarity, hundreds of millions of French people around the world are not! How embarrassing that these spectacular, majestic mountains are reduced to a dirty joke overseas." After a flurry of letters in response, the hoax was revealed; it was a prank by staff members of *Spy* magazine.

PLANNING YOUR TIME

Wyoming's preeminent tourist town, Jackson is both an important access point for Yellowstone and Grand Teton National Parks and a destination in its own right. Visitors should probably plan on at least two days, but you could

easily spend a couple of weeks just having fun in Jackson Hole (if your credit card doesn't get maxed out). Jackson has two peak seasons: summer, when families and international travelers stay here as part of a Yellowstone trip, and winter, when skiing and snowboarding are the big draws.

Prior to your trip, contact the Jackson Hole Chamber of Commerce (307/733-3316, www.jacksonholechamber.com) for brochures, or browse their website for links to hundreds of

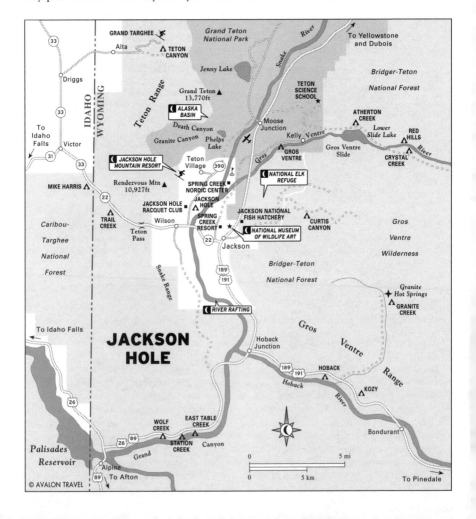

local businesses. Once in town, be sure to drop by the **Jackson Hole & Greater Yellowstone Visitor Center** (532 N. Cache Dr., 307/733-3316, www.jacksonholechamber.com, open daily) for publications, maps, and detailed area information.

Town Square in the heart of Jackson is shady and set with picturesque elk-antler arches on the corners, and a nearby street corner closes for entertaining shoot-outs most summer evenings. Acclaimed as one of the top artistic centers in the nation, Jackson has more than 30 **art galleries,** and the impressive **National Museum of Wildlife Art** perches along a hillside just north of town.

Visitors are drawn to the **National Elk Refuge** for its wintertime sleigh rides among the elk. Skiers and snowboarders enjoy the slopes at famous **Jackson Hole Mountain Resort,** smaller **Snow King Resort,** or on the deep powder of **Grand Targhee Resort,** a morning bus ride away on the west side of the Tetons. Jackson's restaurants are easily the finest (and most expensive) in Wyoming, and lodging varies from cozy old log units to ultra-luxurious hotels. In summer, the **Snake River** is a major center for whitewater rafting and fly-fishing, while mountain bikers and hikers head out on miles of paths. Horseback rides and chuck-wagon cookouts are other summertime favorites, as are the twice-weekly Jackson Hole rodeos. At Teton Village, visitors enjoy classical music performances during the Grand Teton Music Festival in July and August. More adventurous visitors head out on extended back-country trips into Grand Teton National Park and national forest lands, including beautiful **Alaska Basin** on the west side of the Tetons.

Jackson

The town of Jackson (pop. 9,000) lies near the southern end of Jackson Hole, hemmed in on three sides by Snow King Mountain, the Gros Ventre Range, and East Gros Ventre Butte. At 6,200 feet in elevation, Jackson experiences cold, snowy winters, wet springs, delightfully warm and sunny summers, and crisp, color-filled falls. Jackson is unlike any other place in Wyoming; on a typical summer day more than 35,000 tourists flood the town. Sit on a bench in Town Square on a summer day and you're likely to see cars from every state in the country. Tourists dart in and out of the many gift shops, art galleries, fine restaurants, Western-style saloons, and trendy boutiques. The cowboy hats all look as if the price tags just came off.

In other parts of Wyoming, Jackson is viewed with a mixture of awe and disdain—awe over its gorgeous scenery, but disdain that Jackson is not a "real" town, just a false front put up to sell things to outsiders. Yes, Jackson is almost wholly dependent on the almighty tourist dollar, but as a result it enjoys a cultural richness lacking in other parts of the state. Besides, if you don't like all the commercial foolishness, it's easy to escape to a campsite or remote trail in the wonderful countryside of nearby Grand Teton National Park or Bridger-Teton National Forest.

Keep your eyes open around Jackson and you're likely to see well-known residents such as Hollywood stars Harrison Ford and Calista Flockhart, Danny DeVito and Rhea Perlman, Connie Stevens, and Sandra Bullock, along with former Secretary of the Interior James Watt (who resigned in disgrace in 1983), attorney Gerald Spence (of Karen Silkwood and Imelda Marcos notoriety), Yvon Chouinard (mountaineer and founder of Patagonia), industrial heir Charles DuPont, and members of the extended Rockefeller family. Former Vice President Dick Cheney has a luxury home in Teton Pines and is a frequent visitor, which explains all of the Blackhawk helicopters, Secret Service agents, and Suburbans with dark-tinted windows.

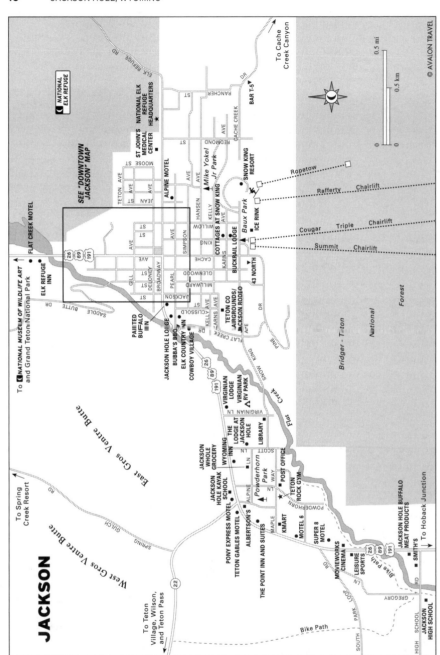

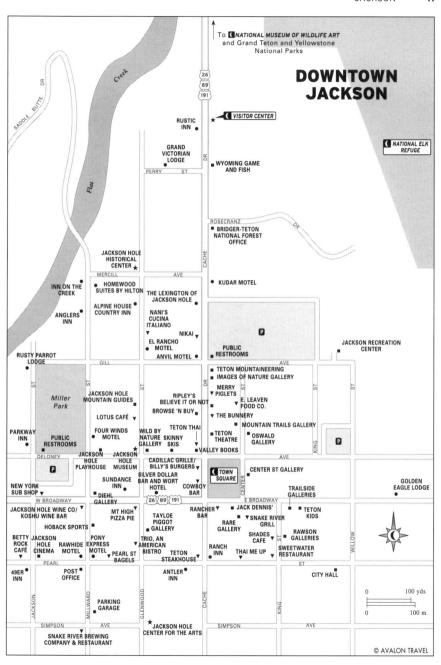

To **(** NATIONAL MUSEUM OF WILDLIFE ART
and Grand Teton and Yellowstone
National Parks

DOWNTOWN JACKSON

(VISITOR CENTER

(NATIONAL ELK REFUGE

RUSTIC INN

GRAND VICTORIAN LODGE

PERRY ST

■ WYOMING GAME AND FISH

ROSECRANZ

■ BRIDGER-TETON NATIONAL FOREST OFFICE

JACKSON HOLE HISTORICAL CENTER ★

MERCILL AVE

● KUDAR MOTEL

INN ON THE CREEK

● HOMEWOOD SUITES BY HILTON

THE LEXINGTON OF JACKSON HOLE

ALPINE HOUSE ● COUNTRY INN

NANI'S CUCINA ITALIANO

ANGLERS INN

▼ NIKAI ▼

EL RANCHO MOTEL ●

ANVIL MOTEL ●

PUBLIC RESTROOMS ■

JACKSON RECREATION CENTER ■

RUSTY PARROT LODGE ●

GILL

AVE

■ TETON MOUNTAINEERING
■ IMAGES OF NATURE GALLERY

Miller Park

JACKSON HOLE MOUNTAIN GUIDES ●

RIPLEY'S BELIEVE IT OR NOT ■

MERRY ▼ PIGLETS

E. LEAVEN FOOD CO. ▼

PARKWAY INN ●

LOTUS CAFÉ ●

BROWSE 'N BUY ■

▼ THE BUNNERY

PUBLIC RESTROOMS ■

FOUR WINDS ● MOTEL

WILD BY NATURE GALLERY

TETON THAI ▼ SKINNY SKIS

■ MOUNTAIN TRAILS GALLERY

■ TETON THEATRE

■ OSWALD GALLERY

DELONEY

▼ VALLEY BOOKS

AVE

JACKSON HOLE PLAYHOUSE

JACKSON HOLE MUSEUM

CADILLAC GRILLE/ BILLY'S BURGERS ▼

★ **(** TOWN SQUARE

■ CENTER ST GALLERY

NEW YORK SUB SHOP ▼

SUNDANCE INN ●

SILVER DOLLAR BAR AND WORT HOTEL

COWBOY BAR

TRAILSIDE GALLERIES

GOLDEN EAGLE LODGE

W BROADWAY

■ DIEHL GALLERY

26 89 191

E BROADWAY

JACKSON HOLE WINE CO/ KOSHU WINE BAR ▼

MT HIGH PIZZA PIE

RANCHER ▼ BAR

■ JACK DENNIS'

■ TETON KIDS

HOBACK SPORTS ■

TAYLOE PIGGOT GALLERY

RARE GALLERY

▼ SNAKE RIVER GRILL

■ RAWSON GALLERIES

BETTY ROCK CAFÉ ▼

JACKSON HOLE CINEMA

RAWHIDE MOTEL

PONY EXPRESS MOTEL

TRIO, AN AMERICAN BISTRO

SHADES ▼ CAFÉ

SWEETWATER RESTAURANT

▼ PEARL ST BAGELS

TETON STEAKHOUSE ▼

RANCH INN

THAI ME UP ▼

PEARL

49ER ● INN

POST OFFICE ■

ANTLER INN

CITY HALL ■

JACKSON

MILLWARD

PARKING GARAGE

GLENWOOD

CACHE

KING

SIMPSON AVE

SIMPSON AVE

★ JACKSON HOLE CENTER FOR THE ARTS

SNAKE RIVER BREWING COMPANY & RESTAURANT

0   100 yds

0   100 m

© AVALON TRAVEL

◖ VISITOR CENTER

Anyone new to Jackson Hole should be sure to visit the spacious **Jackson Hole and Greater Yellowstone Visitor Center** (532 N. Cache Dr., 307/733-3316, www.jacksonholechamber.com, daily 8 A.M.–7 P.M. late May–early Sept., 9 A.M.–5 P.M. the rest of the year) on the north side of town. (The phone is answered only on weekdays, but on weekends you can leave a message and you'll be mailed an information packet.)

The information center is a two-level, sod-roofed wooden building—jokingly called the "little prairie on the house"—with natural-history displays, a blizzard of free leaflets extolling the merits of local businesses, a gift shop selling regional books and maps, and a covered upstairs deck overlooking the National Elk Refuge. Ducks and trumpeter swans are visible on the marsh in the summer, and elk can be seen in the winter. Downstairs, the "bear cave" is a big kid draw. The information center is staffed by the Jackson Hole Chamber of Commerce, along with Fish and Wildlife Service, Forest Service, and other agency personnel in the summer. Free nature and history talks are generally given several times a week during the summer, or you can watch a video about the refuge.

In addition to the main information center, you'll find brochure racks at the airport, the stagecoach stop on Town Square, next to the public restrooms at Cache and Gill, and the Mangy Moose in Teton Village.

◖ TOWN SQUARE

In 1932, the local Rotary Club planted trees in the center of Jackson, adding four picturesque arches made from hundreds of elk antlers in the 1950s and 1960s. Today the trees offer summertime shade, and at any time of day or night you'll find visitors admiring or posing for photos in front of the arches that mark the corners of Town Square. During winter, the snow-covered arches and trees are draped with lights, giving the square a festive atmosphere. Surrounded by dozens of boardwalk-fronted galleries, bars, restaurants, factory outlets, and

stagecoach at Town Square, downtown Jackson

© KATHY ERICKSON / WILD ABOUT LIFE PHOTOGRAPHY

JACKSON HOLE IN 1835

This Valley is called "Jackson Hole" it is generally from 5 to 15 mls wide: the southern part where the river enters the mountain is hilly and uneven but the Northern portion is wide smooth and comparatively even the whole being covered with wild sage and Surrounded by high and rugged mountains upon whose summits the snow remains during the hottest months in Summer. The alluvial bottoms along the river and streams inter sect it thro. the valley produce a luxuriant groth of vegetation among which wild flax and a species of onion are abundant. The great altitude of this place however connected with the cold descending from the mountains at night I think would be a serious obstruction to growth of most Kinds of cultivated grains. This valley like all other parts of the country abounds with game.

Osborne Russell,
Journal of a Trapper 1834-1843

ART

Artists have long been attracted by the beauty of Jackson Hole and the Tetons. Mount Moran, the 12,605-foot summit behind Jackson Lake, is named for Thomas Moran, whose watercolors helped persuade Congress to set aside Yellowstone as the first national park. The late Conrad Schwiering's paintings of the Tetons have attained international fame; one was even used on the Postal Service's Wyoming Centennial stamp in 1990. Ansel Adams's photograph of the Tetons remains etched in the American consciousness as one of the archetypal wilderness images. A copy of the image was included in the payload of the *Voyager II* spacecraft en route out of our solar system. Today many artists live or work in Jackson Hole, and locals proclaim it "Art Center of the Rockies," ranking it with New York, San Francisco, Santa Fe, and Scottsdale.

Jackson Hole Center for the Arts

If you have any doubts that Jackson Hole is an arts mecca, look no further than the modern Jackson Hole Center for the Arts (240 S. Glenwood, 307/734-8956, www.jhcenterforthearts.org). This 41,000-square-foot masterpiece has space for 15 different nonprofit arts organizations under one roof, with an amazing array of classes and workshops. Drop by to pick up a schedule of classes. Newly added in 2007, the 525-seat **Performing Arts Pavilion** is a lovely performance space. Call the box office for tickets, 307/733-4900, or find the online calendar of upcoming performances.

One of the primary tenants is the **Art Association** (307/733-6379, www.artassociation.org), offering dozens of classes and workshops year-round in everything from photography and ceramics to stained glass and woodworking. The on-site **ArtSpace Gallery** displays changing exhibitions by regional and national artists.

Dancer's Workshop (307/733-6398, www.dwjh.org) occupies much of the second floor, with dozens of classes weekly in modern, ballet, pointe, hip-hop, ballroom, jazz, country-and-western, and other dance forms. The facilities

gift shops, the square is the focal point of tourist activity in Jackson.

During summer, **stagecoaches** wait to transport you on a leisurely ride around town, and each evening "cowboys" put on a free **shoot-out** for throngs of camera-happy tourists. The shoot-out starts at 6:15 P.M. Monday–Saturday nights all summer. They've been killing each other like this since 1957. With stereotypical players and questionable acting, the "mountain law" system seems in dire need of reform. Most folks love the sham; Canon and Olympus love it even more. Warning: The sound of blanks is surprisingly loud and can be frightening for small children.

Jackson Hole Center for the Arts

also house Contemporary Dance Wyoming, the state's only professional dance company.

Also at the Center for the Arts, **Off Square Theatre Company** (307/733-3670, www.off-square.org) is a professional repertory company with comedies in the summer and a wide variety of productions and workshops throughout the winter.

◖ NATIONAL MUSEUM OF WILDLIFE ART

Jackson is home to the magnificent National Museum of Wildlife Art (307/733-5771 or 800/313-9553, www.wildlifeart.org), two miles north of town along U.S. Highway 26/89 and directly across from the National Elk Refuge. A monumental sculpture of five elk greets visitors at the base of the hill, and the building's Arizona sandstone exterior blends in with nearby rock outcroppings. Step inside the doors of this 51,000-square-foot museum to discover a marvelous interior. As visitors enter the main gallery, a larger-than-life bronze mountain lion crouches

above, ready to pounce. Kids will have fun in the hands-on Children's Discovery Gallery and can join hands-in-the-paint activities on Monday mornings. Adults will appreciate the artwork spread throughout a dozen galleries, along with the video theater, Rising Sage Café (tasty lunches), 200-seat auditorium, and gift shop. Cyclists and those on foot can access the museum from an underpass beneath the highway that connects with the bike path to Jackson. A sculpture garden is scheduled for completion in 2012.

The museum collection features pieces by Carl Rungius, George Catlin, Albert Bierstadt, Karl Bodmer, Alfred Jacob Miller, N. C. Wyeth, Conrad Schwiering, John Clymer, Charles Russell, Robert Bateman, and many others. Of particular interest are the reconstructed studio of John Clymer and the spacious Carl Rungius Gallery, where you'll find the most complete collection of Clymer's paintings in the nation. Also of note is the exhibit on American bison, which documents these once vastly abundant animals and their slaughter;

ART GALLERIES

More than 30 galleries crowd the center of Jackson. As the town has grown, local galleries have also evolved. You'll still find places selling ludicrously romanticized cowboy paintings and campy prints of sexy Indian maidens with windblown hair and strategically torn garments, but the town is increasingly filled with galleries that exhibit sophisticated and contemporary works.

The **Jackson Hole Gallery Association** (www.jacksonholegalleries.com) produces a helpful gallery guide; pick up one from local galleries or the visitor center. **Third Thursday Art Walks** are a monthly staple, when many galleries open for extended evening hours June–October. Tammy Christel of **Jackson Hole Art Tours** (307/690-1983, www.jacksonholearttours.com) leads informative gallery tours.

Excellent galleries with changing exhibits of modern art are **RARE Gallery** (60 E. Broadway, 2nd floor, 307/733-8726, www.raregalleryjacksonhole.com), **Diehl Gallery** (155 W. Broadway, 307/733-0905, www.diehlgallery.com), **Tayloe Piggott Gallery** (62 S. Glenwood St., 307/733-0555, www.tayloepiggottgallery.com), **Altamira Fine Art** (172 Center St., 307/739-4700, www.altamiraart.com), and **Teton Artlab** (307/699-0836, www.tetonartlab.com) inside the Center for the Arts at 240 S. Glenwood. All are well worth a visit, as is **Wild Hands** (265 W. Pearl Ave., 307/733-4619, www.wildhands.com), with functional and playful art and pottery.

In a quiet spot just a block off Town Square, the two-level **Trailside Galleries** (130 E. Broadway, 307/733-3186, www.trailsidegalleries.com) displays everything from grandiose Western works to impressionist and wildlife art. Other traditionalist galleries worth a look are **Mountain Trails Gallery** (150 N. Center St.,

307/734-8150, www.mtntrails.net), **Legacy Gallery** (75 N. Cache, 307/733-2353, www.legacygallery.com), **Joanne Hennes Gallery** (5850 N. Larkspur Dr., 307/733-2593, www.joannehennes.com), and **Wilcox Gallery** (165 Center St., 307/733-3950, www.wilcoxgallery.com).

Rawson Galleries (50 King St., 307/733-7306) features traditional watercolors, displayed in a crowded space; open July–October.

For a very different type of art, visit **By Nature Gallery** (86 E. Broadway, 307/200-6060, www.bynaturegallery.com), where unique furnishings have been created from fossilized fish, minerals, and more.

PHOTO GALLERIES

Many nationally known photographers live or work in Jackson Hole. Tom Mangelsen displays his outstanding wildlife and landscape photos at **Images of Nature Gallery** (170 N. Cache Dr., 307/733-9752 or 888/238-0177, www.mangelsen.com) and has galleries at 15 other locations around the country.

Inside **Wild by Nature Gallery** (95 W. Deloney, 307/733-8877 or 888/494-5329, www.wildbynature.com), photographer Henry H. Holdsworth shows strikingly beautiful wildlife and nature imagery.

In Gaslight Alley at 125 North Cache, **Brookover Gallery** (307/733-3988, www.brookovergallery.com) exhibits grandiose landscapes by photographer David Brookover, who works with an 8x10 camera.

At **Oswald Gallery** (165 N. Center St., 888/898-0077, www.oswaldgallery.com) the emphasis is on contemporary fine-art photography. There's always something visually challenging; this isn't the place to look for pretty nature scenes.

the museum's bison collection is the largest in the world. Six galleries showcase photography, painting, and other art that changes throughout the year. Spotting scopes in the cozy members' lounge (open to the public) are useful for

watching residents of the adjacent National Elk Refuge.

Museum admission is $12 adults, $10 seniors, $6 ages 5–18; free for kids under five. Hours are daily 9 A.M.–5 P.M. in summer, and 9 A.M.–5 P.M. Monday–Saturday and 11 A.M.–5 P.M. Sunday mid-October–April. The museum is closed Christmas, Thanksgiving, and Columbus Day. Free audio tours detail works in the permanent collection, and you can watch films on wildlife.

Wildlife films, slide lectures, talks, concerts, kids' programs, and other activities take place throughout the year in the auditorium and galleries; pick up a schedule of upcoming events at the entrance desk or visit the museum website. One of the most popular events, **Western Visions,** comes in late September. It includes jewelry, photography, and the Miniature Show & Sale, with small works by 100 of the country's leading artists. A winter highlight is **Art After Hours/ Tapas Tuesdays** (5–9 P.M. Tues., Dec.–Mar.), when the museum opens for après-ski programs combined with tapas served by Rising Sage Café.

HISTORICAL MUSEUMS

The small **Jackson Hole Museum** (105 N. Glenwood, 307/733-2414, www.jacksonhole-history.org, noon–5 P.M. Sun., 10 A.M.–6 P.M. Mon.–Sat. late May–mid-Sept., closed the rest of the year) has a surprising homespun charm. Inside are displays and collections illustrating the days when Indians, trappers, cattlemen, and dude ranchers called this magnificent valley home. Check out the rock-encrusted flintlock musket, the old postcards, and a replica of the "Colter stone." Admission is $3 adults, $2 seniors, $1 ages 3–18, and $6 families. In the summer, the museum sponsors free hour-long **historical walking tours** of Jackson's downtown on Tuesdays and Thursdays at 10:30 A.M.

Also managed by the local historical society, the **Jackson Hole Historical Center** (105 Mercill Ave., 307/733-9605, 10 A.M.–5 P.M. Tues.–Fri. year-round, free) is a small research facility housing photo archives, a library of classic regional books, and rotating exhibits throughout the year.

◀ NATIONAL ELK REFUGE

Immediately north of Jackson is the National Elk Refuge (307/733-9212, www.fws.gov/nationalelkrefuge), winter home for thousands of these majestic animals. During summer, the elk range up to 65 miles away to feed on grasses, shrubs, and forbs in alpine meadows. But as the snows descend each fall, they move downslope, wintering in Jackson Hole and the surrounding country. The chance to view elk up close from a horse-drawn sleigh makes a trip to the National Elk Refuge one of the most popular wintertime activities for Jackson Hole visitors.

History

When the first ranchers arrived in Jackson Hole in the late 19th century, they moved onto land that had long been an elk migration route and wintering ground. The ranchers soon found elk raiding their haystacks and competing with cattle for forage, particularly during severe winters. The conflicts peaked early in the 20th century when three consecutive severe winters killed thousands of elk, leading one settler to claim that he had "walked for a mile on dead elk lying from one to four deep." Following a national outcry, the federal government began buying land in 1911 for a permanent winter elk refuge that would eventually cover nearly 25,000 acres.

About 5,500 elk (two-thirds of the local population) typically spend November–May on the refuge, administered by the U.S. Fish and Wildlife Service. Because development has reduced elk habitat in the valley to one-quarter of its original size, refuge managers try to improve the remaining land through seeding, irrigation, and prescribed burning. In addition, during the most difficult foraging period, the elk are fed alfalfa pellets paid for in part by sales of elk antlers collected on the refuge. During this time, each elk eats more than seven pounds of supplemental alfalfa per day, or 30 tons per day for the entire herd. Elk head back into the mountains with the melting of snow each April and May; during summer you'll see few (if any) on the refuge.

COURTESY OF JACKSON HOLE CHAMBER OF COMMERCE

elk with sleigh, National Elk Refuge

Visiting the Refuge

The National Elk Refuge is primarily a winter attraction, although it's also an excellent place to watch birds and other wildlife—including nesting trumpeter swans—in summer. Refuge staff are on duty year-round in the Jackson Hole & Greater Yellowstone Visitor Center (532 N. Cache Dr., 307/733-3316, www.jacksonhole-chamber.com, open daily), leading nature talks, summertime wildlife viewing from the back deck, and theater programs. Visit the picturesque and historic (built in 1898) **Miller Ranch** on the east side of the refuge, 0.75 mile out Elk Refuge Road. It's open daily 10 A.M.–4 P.M. Memorial Day–Labor Day, with a naturalist available to answer questions about the refuge.

The main winter attraction here is the chance to see thousands of elk up close from one of the **horse-drawn sleighs** that take visitors through the refuge. The elk are accustomed to these sleighs and pay little heed, but people on foot would scare them. A tour of the National Elk Refuge is always a highlight for wintertime visitors to Jackson Hole. In December and January the bulls have impressive antlers

that they start to shed by the end of February. The months of January and February are good times to see sparring matches. You might also catch a glimpse of a wolf or two, because a pack now lives in the area year-round and hunts elk in winter. Morning is the best time to look for wolves.

Begin your wintertime visit to the refuge at the Jackson Hole & Greater Yellowstone Visitor Center, where you can buy sleigh-ride tickets ($18 adults, $14 ages 5–12, free for kids under age five). Reservations are available, but are not required, through Bar-T-Five (307/733-0277 or 800/772-5386, www.bart5.com), the folks who run the sleighs. The visitor center shows an interpretive slide show about the refuge while you're waiting for a shuttle bus to take you to the boarding area. Sleighs run daily 10 A.M.–4 P.M. mid-December–March (closed Christmas), heading out as soon as enough folks show up for a ride—generally just long enough for the early-comers to finish watching the slide show. The rides last 45–60 minutes. Be sure to wear warm clothes or bring extra layers, because the wind can get bitterly cold.

Hatchery

Four miles north of town and adjacent to the elk refuge is the **Jackson National Fish Hatchery** (307/733-2510, http://jackson. fws.gov, daily 8 A.M.–4 P.M. year-round), which rears 400,000 cutthroat trout annually. There's also a small pond open for fishing on the grounds (fishing license required), a great spot for kids and novice anglers.

RAPTOR CENTER

Teton Raptor Center (307/203-2551, www. tetonraptorcenter.org, noon–4 P.M. Tues. and Thurs., 8 A.M.–noon Wed. in summer) is housed within the historic red barns of the Hardeman Ranch, seven miles from Jackson in the little town of Wilson. The center rehabilitates injured birds of prey and offers tours (by appointment, $10) several times weekly in the summer. This is a great chance for an up-close view of a golden eagle, red-tail hawk, and various falcons. The center also offers free weekly evening talks at Teton Village; their website features an osprey cam for live summer action on a nearby nest.

KITSCH

If you're a fan of the *National Enquirer,* check out the weird and wacky collection at **Ripley's Believe It or Not!** (140 N. Cache, 307/734-0000, www.conceptattractions.com, daily 9 A.M.–10 P.M. in summer, and noon–6 P.M. Sun., 11 A.M.–7 P.M. Mon.–Thurs., 10 A.M.–8 P.M. Fri.–Sat. the rest of the year; closed Tues.–Wed. Nov.–Dec.). Here you'll discover a shrunken head, six-legged buffalo calf, six-foot-long cigar, antique bedpan collection, and even art created from dryer lint. Who says art is only for the elite? Entrance costs a steep $11 adults, $9 ages 5–12, free for kids under five.

For more foolishness, have the kids drag you to the **Teton Maze** (307/734-0455) across from the Snow King chairlift. As the ads proclaim, it's a-Maze-ing.

Summer Recreation

Summer visitors to Jackson Hole can choose from an overwhelming array of outdoor options. Top favorites include float trips and whitewater rafting on the Snake River, mountain biking, hiking, and horseback rides, but kids love the alpine slide at Snow King, the fun pool at the rec center, and the tram rides at Jackson Hole Resort, not to mention the Town Square shoot-outs and evening rodeos that fill the summer calendar. If you've booked only a few days, you'll wish for more time to explore this fascinating place.

HIKING

The country around Jackson abounds with hundreds of miles of hiking trails, providing recreation opportunities for all levels of ability. Many of the most popular local trails are within nearby **Grand Teton National Park.** Notable in-the-park hikes are found in the Taggart Lake and Jenny Lake areas, at Colter Bay, and off the Moose-Wilson Road. The Information Center in Jackson has a brochure detailing these hikes, and a local outdoors shop, Skinny Skis (65 W. Deloney Ave., 307/733-6094 or 888/733-7205, www.skinnyskis.com), produces an excellent free summertime guide to hiking in the area called *Trailhead.*

For a fast trip to the alpine, take the **Jackson Hole Ski Resort tram** to the summit of Rendezvous Mountain ($25 adults, $12 kids), where trails fan out in various directions into Grand Teton National Park; the bird's-eye view is hard to beat. Visitors can also ride the free **Bridger gondola** (4:30–9 P.M.) to the 9,095-foot level, with access to additional hiking trails, as well as casual meals at the Deck or fine dining at Couloir Restaurant.

Snow King

Closest to town are the trails at Snow King (400 E. Snow King Ave., 307/733-5200 or 800/522-

5464, www.snowking.com), where you can either hike up the mountain or ride the chairlift ($12) to the summit and hike back down. Once on top, you'll find a 0.5-mile nature trail and wonderful across-the-valley views of the Tetons. Nearby is the **Cache Creek Trail,** which follows this pretty creek uphill for six miles along an old road that's closed to motor vehicles. It's a great family hike or mountain-bike ride. For an alternate loop back (four miles round-trip), turn onto the **Putt-Putt Trail** two miles up. Cyclists often use Cache Creek Trail to connect with Game Creek Trail for a loop around Snow King Mountain. All of the trails in the Snow King area are open to mountain bikes, and you can transport bikes on the chairlift.

Teton Pass

Ski Lake is a more challenging hike or bike ride, with spectacular views awaiting. It starts west of Wilson on Highway 22 at Phillips Canyon. Walk up the dirt road 0.5 mile and take the left fork in the road to the start of the trail. It side-slopes around to a viewpoint and then climbs through the forest to Ski Lake, nestled high in the alpine and three miles from your starting point. The **Black Canyon Overlook Trail** starts from the parking area at the top of Teton Pass, 10 miles west of Jackson. It follows Pass Ridge for two miles, with an abundance of wildflower meadows and forest along the way. You can continue from here down Black Canyon to the end of Trail Creek Road at the base of the pass for a longer hike, but will need a shuttle ride back up the pass.

Snake River Canyon

The Snake River Canyon south of Jackson is best known as a river-rafting destination, but a couple of good hikes are a landlubber's option. The **Cabin Creek Trail** begins 0.5 mile up a dirt road behind Cabin Creek Campground (17 miles from Jackson). The trail follows the creek uphill to a pass that is filled with late-summer wildflowers, and from here you'll be treated to delightful views of the Snake River drainage. Return the same way, or head back downhill along the **Dog Creek Trail** that ends near the junction of Wilson-Fall Creek Road with U.S. Highway 89/26. Either way, it's about six miles of hiking, but if you head back via Dog Creek Trail you'll need a shuttle back to your car.

Granite Creek

This beautiful valley has good hiking, a quiet out-of-the-way location, and the added bonus of a hot spring. Get here by driving south from Jackson 12 miles to Hoback Junction and then another 12 miles east on U.S. Highway 189 to the turnoff for Granite Hot Springs. The **Granite Creek Falls Trail** starts at the junction of Swift Creek and Granite Creek, eight miles up the road. It follows the creek upstream to impressive Granite Falls and then on to **Granite Hot Springs** (also accessible by road), where you can soak in the wonderful mineral pool for $6. Towel and swimsuit rentals are available. The trail is two miles long and quite easy, and there's a campground near the springs.

For a more challenging hike, try the **Shoal Falls Trail,** which starts from the same trailhead eight miles up Granite Creek Road and leads five miles to an overlook near Shoal Falls. Get trail details from the Forest Service.

Guided Hikes

Teton County Parks & Recreation Department (155 E. Gill St., 307/739-9025, www.tetonwyo.org/parks) sponsors a wide range of outdoor activities in the summer, including adult day hikes. For a break from the young'uns (1st–6th grade), take them to the **Camp Jackson** summer day camp at Davey Jackson Elementary (200 N. Willow, 307/733-5302), available weekdays for $35 per day. You don't need to be a local resident to take part in any of these activities, but reserve ahead because some fill up. The Parks & Rec office also rents out volleyball, horseshoe, bocce ball, and croquet sets.

Educational nature walks into the mountains around Jackson are led by **The Hole Hiking Experience** (307/690-4453 or 866/733-4453, www.holehike.com). Rates start at $82 adults,

$65 for kids for a four-hour hike. Longer trips, including multi-night backpacking, are also available. For a free version, Grand Teton National Park offers guided walks and nature talks throughout the year.

For a different sort of guided hike, check out the excellent and free **historical walking tours** offered by the Jackson Hole Museum on Tuesday and Thursday.

◖ RIVER RAFTING

Jackson Hole's most popular summertime recreational activity is running Wyoming's largest river, the Snake. Each year more than 150,000 people climb aboard rafts, canoes, and kayaks to float down placid reaches of the Snake or to blast through the boiling rapids of Snake River Canyon. (The name "Snake" comes from the Shoshone Indians, who used serpentine hand movements as sign language for their tribal name—a motion trappers misinterpreted as a snake and applied to the river flowing through Shoshone land.)

Almost 20 different rafting companies offer dozens of raft trips each day of the summer. Although you may be able to walk up and get a raft trip the same day, it's a good idea to reserve ahead for any river trip in July and August. In general, try to book a trip three or four days in advance and at least one week ahead if you need a specific time, prefer an overnight float trip, or are traveling with a larger group. One or two people are more likely to get onboard at the last minute.

You may want to ask around to determine the advantages of each company. Some are cheaper but require you to drive a good distance from town; others offer more experienced crews; still others provide various perks such as fancy meals, U-paddle trips, overnight camps along the river, interpretive trips, or boats with fewer (or more) people. Several operators also lead seven-hour combination trips that include a lazy float followed by a meal break and a wild whitewater run.

The rafting companies generally operate mid-May–late September, and river conditions change throughout the season. Highest flows—and the wildest rides—are generally in May and June. Get a complete list of floating and boating outfits, along with descriptive brochures, from the visitor center in Jackson.

Float Trips

The gentlest way to see the Snake is by taking one of the many commercial float trips. Along the way, you'll be treated to stunning views of the Tetons and glimpses of eagles, ospreys, beavers, and perhaps moose or other wildlife along the riverbanks. Several companies—Barker-Ewing Float Trips, Will Dornan's Snake River Float Trips, Grand Teton Lodge Company, Signal Mountain, Solitude, and Triangle X—offer 10-mile scenic float trips along the quiet stretch **within Grand Teton National Park,** putting in at Deadman's Bar and taking out at Moose ($55–60 adults, $35–40 kids). (Grand Teton Lodge Company often puts in at Pacific Creek.) Triangle X offers a unique 12-mile park supper float-and-cookout with access to a private spot along the river.

Other rafting companies offer 13-mile **South Park float trips outside the park,** putting in at the bridge near Wilson and taking out above Hoback Junction ($45–60 adults, $40–50 kids, lunch included). Companies offering this trip are Barker-Ewing Whitewater & Scenic, Dave Hansen, Lewis & Clark, Sands, Will Dornan's Snake River Float Trips, Jackson Hole Whitewater, Snake River Kayak & Canoe School, Snake River Park, Solitude, Teton Whitewater, and Teton Expeditions. In-the-park trips are considerably more scenic, so know what you're getting before you sign up since the differences are not emphasized by the rafting companies (at least not by those who don't operate inside the park). Given the choice, I would always choose the trip that passes below the Tetons over the one that skirts suburban Jackson. Some companies add options such as breakfast cookouts or overnight trips with camping along the way.

Age limits vary, but kids must generally be at least eight to float the river. Raft companies usually have folks meet up in either Jackson or Moose. A wide variety of special voyages are also available, including overnight camping and fish-and-float trips.

OUTFITTERS

The following rafting outfits offer a variety of float trips. Pick up their slick brochures at the visitor center or from their offices scattered around town.

- **Barker-Ewing Float Trips** (307/733-1800 or 800/365-1800, www.barkerewing.com)
- **Barker-Ewing Whitewater & Scenic** (307/733-1000 or 800/448-4202, www.barker-ewing.com)
- **Dave Hansen Scenic Float Trips** (307/733-6295 or 800/732-6295, www.davehansenscenicfloattrips.com)
- **Grand Teton Lodge Company** (307/543-3100 or 800/628-9988, www.gtlc.com)
- **Jackson Hole Whitewater** (307/733-1007 or 800/700-7238, www.jhww.com)
- **Lewis & Clark Expeditions** (307/733-4022 or 800/824-5375, www.lewisandclarkriverrafting.com)
- **Mad River Boat Trips** (307/733-6203 or 800/458-7238, www.mad-river.com)
- **Sands Wild Water** (307/733-4410 or 800/358-8184, www.sandswhitewater.com)
- **Signal Mountain Lodge and Marina** (307/543-2831 or 307/543-2831, www.signalmountainlodge.com)
- **Snake River Kayak & Canoe School** (307/733-9999 or 800/529-2501, www.snakeriverkayak.com) Snake River Kayak & Canoe School also has "rubber duckie" inflatable kayaks for a unique whitewater adventure.
- **Snake River Park Whitewater** (307/733-7078 or 800/562-1878, www.snakeriverwhitewater.com)
- **Solitude Scenic Float Trips** (307/733-2871 or 888/704-2800, www.solitudefloattrips.com)
- **Teton Expeditions** (307/733-1007 or 888/700-7238, www.tetonexpeditions.com)
- **Teton Whitewater** (307/733-2285 or 866/716-7238, www.tetonwhitewater.com)
- **Triangle X Float Trips** (a.k.a. National Park Float Trips, 307/733-5500 or 888/860-0005, www.trianglex.com)
- **Will Dornan's Snake River Float Trips** (307/733-3699 or 888/998-7688, www.jacksonholefloattrips.com)

As an aside, one of the oldest names in the business, **Barker-Ewing,** is actually two different operations with rather different agendas. Barker-Ewing originated in 1963 when Dick Barker and Frank Ewing started guiding clients down the Snake River. They went their separate ways in 1984, and today, the Barker family operates Grand Teton National Park float trips under the name Barker-Ewing Float Trips, while the Ewing family runs Snake River whitewater trips and South Park floats under the name Barker-Ewing Whitewater & Scenic. Both companies splash "Barker-Ewing" across the top of their brochures, adding to the confusion for many travelers. Despite any tension between the two companies, both are first-rate operations with some of the most experienced guides anywhere.

You can also float the river with any of the local fishing outfitters and combine angling with drifting downriver. One good company—it gives a really personalized tour—is **Wooden Boat River Tours** (307/732-2628, www.woodboattours.com, $400 for up to three passengers), which has classic wooden dories.

Note that a few of the raft operators are regarded as "training grounds" for other companies; recommended outfits with good records include Barker-Ewing Float Trips, Solitude, Dave Hansen, and Triangle X. Grand Teton Lodge Float Trips often use massive 15-person rafts with two oarsmen. Unfortunately, three people died in a 2006 accident when one of their rafts hit a tree that had been uprooted by high water, throwing all the passengers into the river. Use caution before booking a river trip when the river is running high following a heavy snowpack year.

Whitewater Trips

Below Jackson, the Snake enters the wild Snake River Canyon, a stretch early explorers labeled "the accursed mad river." The usual put-in point for whitewater "rapid-transit" trips is West Table Creek Campground, 26 miles south of Jackson. The take-out point is Sheep Gulch, eight miles downstream. In between, the river rocks and rolls through the narrow canyon, pumping past waterfalls and eagle nests and then over the two biggest rapids, Big Kahuna and Lunch Counter, followed by the smaller Rope and Champagne rapids. For a look at the action from the highway, stop at the paved turnout at milepost 124, where a trail leads down to Lunch Counter. The river changes greatly throughout the season, with the highest water and wildest rides in June. By August the water has warmed enough for a quick dip. Be sure to ask your river guide about the Jeep that sits in 60 feet of water below Lunch Counter!

Whitewater trips last about 3.5 hours (including transportation from Jackson) and cost about $60–65 adults, $50–55 children (age limits vary). Seven-hour combination trips covering 21 miles include a float trip, deli lunch, and whitewater run for $94–110 adults, $78–90 kids. You'll find discounted rates early or late in the summer.

One feature to consider is raft size. Many companies use smaller eight-person rafts (often called U-paddle), but trips on 14-person monsters are a few dollars cheaper. The U-paddle versions are more fun than letting the guide do all the work in an oar raft, and the smaller eight-person rafts provide the most challenging—and wettest—runs. Snake River Kayak & Canoe offers two-person "rubber duckie" kayak trips.

Note that this is not exactly a wilderness experience, especially in mid-July, when stretches of the river look like a Los Angeles freeway with traffic jams of rafts, kayaks, inner tubes, and other flotsam and jetsam. The river isn't as crowded on weekdays and early in the morning;

take an 8 A.M. run for the fewest people. Early in the season when the river is high and fast your trip can be quite short, sometimes just 45 minutes on the water.

Don't take a camera along unless it's waterproof; bankside float-tographers are positioned along the biggest rapids to shoot both commercial and private rafters. Stop by **Float-O-Graphs** (130 W. Broadway Ave., 307/733-6453 or 888/478-7427, www.floatographs. com) for a photo from your run. Another company with a similar service is **Snake River Whitewater Photos and Video** (140 N. Cache Dr., 307/733-7015 or 800/948-3426, www. snakeriverphotos.net). Both companies also post photos online.

OUTFITTERS

Most outfitters include round-trip transportation from Jackson. (Prices are a bit lower from Snake River Park Whitewater, but you'll need to drive to their office at Hoback Junction, 13 miles south of town.) Some companies also offer trips that combine an eight-mile scenic float trip through South Park with an eight-mile whitewater trip for about $85–90 adults or $75–80 kids.

Rafting companies provide wet suits and booties, but expect to get wet, so wear lightweight clothes and bring a jacket for the return ride.

The following outfitters offer whitewater raft trips. Recommended companies with good safety records and well-trained staff include Barker-Ewing, Dave Hansen, and Sands. The largest local rafting company, Mad River, has a reputation as a proving ground for novice guides (but its prices are typically lower than those of other operators).

- **Barker-Ewing Whitewater & Scenic** (307/733-1000 or 800/448-4202, www. barker-ewing.com)

- **Dave Hansen Whitewater** (307/733-6295 or 800/732-6295, www.davehansenwhitewater.com)

- **Jackson Hole Whitewater** (307/733-1007 or 800/700-7238, www.jhww.com)

- **Lewis & Clark Expeditions** (307/733-4022 or 800/824-5375, www.lewisandclarkriverrafting.com)
- **Mad River Boat Trips** (307/733-6203 or 800/458-7238, www.mad-river.com)
- **Sands Wild Water** (307/733-4410 or 800/358-8184, www.sandswhitewater.com)
- **Snake River Kayak and Canoe School** (307/733-9999 or 800/529-2501, www.snakeriverkayak.com)
- **Snake River Park Whitewater** (307/733-7078 or 800/562-1878, www.snakeriver-whitewater.com)
- **Teton Whitewater** (307/733-2285 or 866/716-7238, www.tetonwhitewater.com)

Riding and Rafts (307/654-9900, www.jacksonholerecreation.com) has raft rentals ($100–115) if you want to float the rapids on your own.

FISHING

Jackson Hole has some of the finest angling in Wyoming, with native Snake River cutthroat (a distinct subspecies) and brook trout in the river, along with Mackinaw (lake trout), cutthroat, and brown trout in the lakes. The Snake is a particular favorite of beginning fly-fishing enthusiasts; popular shoreside fishing spots are just below Jackson Lake Dam and near the Wilson Bridge. Jackson Lake may provide higher odds for catching a fish, but you'll need to rent a boat from one of the marinas. This is the place parents take kids. Another very popular fishing hole is just below the dam on Jackson Lake. Flat Creek on the National Elk Refuge is an acclaimed spot for fly-fishing. Note that Wyoming fishing licenses are valid within Grand Teton National Park but not in Yellowstone, where you'll need a separate permit.

A variety of exotic plants and animals may threaten the Snake River and other waterways, including New Zealand mud snails, zebra mussels, and Eurasian water-milfoil. Help prevent the spread of these pests by carefully cleaning boots, clothing, waders, gear, and boats. More information is available online at www.cleaninspectdry.com and www.protectyourwaters.net.

Fishing Guides

Many local companies guide fly-fishing float trips down the Snake River and other area waterways. Two people (same price for one person) should expect to pay $400–450 per day for a guide, rods and reels, lunch, and boat. Your fishing license and flies are extra. The visitor center has a listing of local fishing guides and outfitters, and its racks are filled with their brochures. You'll also find links to many of these at www.jacksonholechamber.com.

On Your Own

If you'd rather do it yourself, pick up a copy of the free *Jack Dennis Sports Fly Fishing Guide,* which offers descriptions of regional fishing areas and advice on which lures to try. Find it at **Jack Dennis Sports** (50 E. Broadway Ave., 307/733-3270 or 800/570-3270, www.jackdennisoutdoors.com). While there, you may want to buy a regional guide to fishing such as *Flyfisher's Guide to Wyoming* by Ken Retallic (Wilderness Adventures Press, www.wildadvpress.com) or *Fishing Wyoming* by Kenneth Lee Graham (Falcon Guides, www.falcon.com).

Jackson has several excellent fly-fishing shops, including the aforementioned Jack Dennis Sports. **Westbank Anglers** (3670 Teton Village Rd., 307/733-6483 or 800/922-3474, www.westbank.com) is a nationally known fly-fishing dealer with a slick mail-order catalog, excellent fishing clinics, and float trips. **High Country Flies** (185 N. Center St., 307/733-7210 or 866/733-7210, www.highcountryflies.com), **Orvis Jackson Hole** (485 W. Broadway Ave., 307/733-5407, www.orvis.com/jacksonhole), and **Will Dornan's Snake River Angler** (in Moose, 307/733-3699 or 888/998-7688, www.snakeriverangler.com) all offer fly-fishing classes and sell quality gear. Rent fishing rods, fly rods, float tubes, and waders from Jack Dennis, High Country Flies, or **Leisure Sports** (1075 S. U.S. Hwy. 89, 307/733-3040, www.leisuresportsadventure.com).

BOATING
Kayaking and Canoeing

In business for more than 35 years, **Snake River Kayak & Canoe School** (365 N. Cache, 307/733-9999 or 800/529-2501, www.snakeriverkayak.com) offers a wide variety of river kayaking and canoeing classes for all levels of ability, plus fishing trips and raft trips. Half-day private lessons include transportation, boats, paddles, wet suit, rubber bootie, and life jackets ($250 for two students). Beginners may want to start out with one of the three-hour "rubber duckie" inflatable kayak river trips ($75). In addition, the school has sea kayak tours of all lengths in Yellowstone National Park. The shop rents practically anything that floats: canoes, sea kayaks, whitewater kayaks, inflatable kayaks, and rafts, all with paddles and roof racks included. Also available are dry bags and life jackets.

The folks at **Rendezvous River Sports/ Jackson Hole Kayak School** (945 W. Broadway Ave., 307/733-2471, www.jackson-holekayak.com) teach a wide range of kayaking courses from the absolute beginner level to advanced "hairboating" for experts. Classes include kayak roll clinics, river rescue, special women's clinics, and kids' classes, plus multi-day tours in Yellowstone. Private lessons are available, and the company rents sea kayaks and whitewater kayaks, plus inflatable kayaks and rafts.

Leisure Sports (1075 S. U.S. Hwy. 89, 307/733-3040, www.leisuresportsadventure.com) rents rafts, float tubes, canoes, inflatable kayaks, water skis, wet suits, dry bags, life vests, and all sorts of other outdoor equipment. Next to Dornan's in Moose, **Adventure Sports** (307/733-3307, www.dornans.com) also rents canoes and kayaks.

HORSEBACK RIDING
Trail Rides

Think of the Wild West and one animal always comes to mind—the horse. A ride on Old Paint gives city slickers a chance to saunter back in time to a simpler era and to simultaneously learn how ornery and opinionated horses can

be. If it rains, you'll also learn why cowboys are so enthralled with cowboy hats. In Jackson Hole you can choose from brief half-day trail rides in Grand Teton National Park all the way up to weeklong pack trips into the rugged Teton Wilderness. The visitor center has a brochure listing local outfitters and stables that provide trail rides and pack trips.

For rides by the hour or day ($30–40 for a one-hour ride, $45–60 for two hours, or $80–110 for a half-day), try **Teton Village Trail Rides** (in Teton Village, 307/733-2674, www.wagonswestwyo.com), **Jackson Hole Trail Rides** (behind Snow King Resort, 307/733-6992, www.jhtrailrides.com), **Spring Creek Ranch** (atop Gros Ventre Butte off Spring Gulch Road, 307/733-8833 or 800/443-6139, www.springcreekranch.com), **A/OK Corral** (in Hoback Junction, 307/733-6556, www.horsecreekranch.com), **Mill Iron Ranch** (10 miles south of Jackson, 307/733-6390 or 888/808-6390, www.millironranch.net), or **Goosewing Ranch** (25 miles east of Kelly near the Gros Ventre Wilderness, 307/733-5251 or 888/733-5251, www.goosewingranch.com).

Of these, Teton Village Trail Rides, Spring Creek Ranch, and Mill Iron Ranch are the most popular, but you probably won't go wrong with any of these companies. Mill Iron Ranch, Spring Creek Ranch, and A/OK Corral also offer rides that include breakfast or dinner cookouts. Farther afield are several companies offering trail rides, including four that operate out of Buffalo Valley (45 miles northeast of Jackson): **Buffalo Valley Ranch** (307/543-2062 or 888/543-2477, www.buffalovalleyranch.com), **Castagno Outfitters** (307/543-2407 or 877/559-3585, www.castagnooutfitters.com), **Turpin Meadow Ranch** (307/543-2496 or 800/743-2496, www.turpinmeadowranch.com), **Teton Horseback Adventures** (307/730-8829, www.horsebackadv.com), and **Yellowstone Outfitters** (307/543-2418 or 800/447-4711, www.yellowstoneoutfitters.com). More trail rides are offered at **Togwotee Mountain Lodge** (307/543-2847 or 800/543-2847, www.togwoteelodge.com), 48 miles northeast of Jackson on the way to

Togwotee Pass. The minimum age for horseback riding is typically 5–6; young children ride while the horse is being led around by a parent. Teton Village Trail Rides also offers unique **winter rides** at Teton Village ($55 for one hour on plowed trails).

In Alpine (35 miles southwest of Jackson), **Riding and Rafts** (307/654-9900, www.jacksonholerecreation.com) offers unguided horse rentals for $50 for a half-day ride; it's the only local place for do-it-yourselfers. (Pseudo-legal disclaimer from their website: "If you fall off and get hurt, you just have to lie there until you get better.")

Jackson Hole Llamas (307/739-9582 or 800/830-7316, www.jhllamas.com) leads day hikes and backcountry treks with these fascinating and gentle animals.

Chuck-wagon cookouts are a very popular family option in Jackson Hole during the summer. Guests travel in horse-drawn wagons (or by horseback) and are treated to a delicious all-you-can-eat meal and entertainment.

In the foothills eight miles south of Jackson, **Game Creek Ranch** (1500 Game Creek Rd., 307/733-7101, www.gamecreekranch.biz) has a huge indoor riding arena with Western or English riding lessons for all levels, a five-week ranch camp for kids, riding clinics, and horse boarding.

Wagon Trains

Two local companies lead overnight wagon-train rides (in wagons with rubber tires) into the country around Jackson Hole. Guests split their time between riding in the wagons and riding on horseback. **Wagons West** (307/543-2418 or 800/447-4711, www.wagonswestwyo.com) heads up into the Mt. Leidy Highlands for 2–6 days. The shortest trips (two days and one night) are $470 adults, $395 kids under 14. Four-day, three-night trips are $805 adults, $695 kids; and six-day, five-night trips run $1,025 adults, $895 kids. **Teton Wagon Train/ Double H Bar** (307/734-6101 or 888/734-6101, www.tetonwagontrain.com) charges $895 adults, $815 ages 9–14, and $765 ages 4–8 for a four-day, three-night package that includes horseback and wagon riding, meals, and camping gear.

Cowboy for a Day

One of the last working cattle ranches in Jackson Hole, historic **Snake River Ranch** (307/733-2674, www.tetonvillagetrailrides.com) has more than 3,500 head of cattle on a 5,000-acre spread. City slickers can join cowboys as they push cattle between pastures. This is real work and not for the timid, but a great opportunity at $100 for 3–4 hours. The ranch also has wagon tours and is a popular location for weddings.

BIKING

Jackson Hole offers all sorts of adventures for cyclists, particularly those with mountain bikes. Local bike shops provide maps of mountain-bike routes. Note that bikes are not allowed on hiking trails in Grand Teton National Park or in Forest Service wilderness areas. The main road in Grand Teton National Park is plowed but closed to cars and other motorized traffic during April. It's great for an easy and scenic ride.

Bike Paths

Jackson Hole is a wonderful place for bikes, and is fast becoming a destination for cycling enthusiasts, thanks in part to the **Jackson Hole Community Pathways** (307/732-8573, www.tetonwyo.org/pathways). This expanding network of paved paths covers 37 miles, connecting with eight more miles within Grand Teton National Park. Additional trails are being added, and eventually these trails will all be linked, providing continuous bike paths from Hoback Junction north through Grand Teton National Park and west into Teton Valley, Idaho. Visit the Community Pathways website (www.tetonwyo.org/pathways) for details and downloadable maps, or pick up one of their maps at the visitor center. Get additional details from Friends of Pathways (335 S. Millward St., 307/733-4534, www.friendsofpathways.org), a nonprofit advocacy group.

A paved trail heads north from Jackson along

U.S. Highway 26/89/191 into Grand Teton National Park. Built in 2011, the path follows the highway to Moose, where it joins the Park Service's bike path to Jenny Lake. With this connection, it's now possible to bike the entire 21 miles from downtown Jackson to Jenny Lake. Underpasses beneath the highway provide bike and pedestrian access to the National Museum of Wildlife Art and the settlement of Moose in Grand Teton.

A seven-mile paved trail parallels the highway south of Jackson to the Snake River bridge. For a fun loop ride, use this path to connect to the very popular Game Creek Trail, which meets Cache Creek Trail, circling back to Jackson behind Snow King. (Some of this route is not paved.) A paved bike path goes from the town of Wilson westward to the summit of Teton Pass (a gain of 2,000 feet in 3.5 miles), with a second arm continuing from Wilson to Teton Village and then north to Grand Teton National Park parallel to the Moose-Wilson Road. The gap between Jackson and the Snake River should be completed by 2013.

A four-mile path starts behind the main post office on Maple Way, crosses U.S. Highway 89, and continues past the high school before turning north to meet the road to Wilson (Hwy. 22). This road has wide shoulders but gets lots of traffic.

The trails at **Snow King Resort** (400 E. Snow King Ave., 307/733-5200 or 800/522-5464, www.snowking.com) are open to mountain bikers, and you can either pedal uphill or ride the chairlift with your bike ($12). **Jackson Hole Mountain Resort** (307/733-2292 or 888/333-7766, www.jacksonhole.com) has seven miles of bike trails on the lower sections of the mountain for all levels of ability, including a very popular all-downhill bike park with groomed trails, banked corners, and jumps for all levels of ability. Access is via the Teewinot chairlift ($10 adults, $6 kids); no charge if you've purchased a separate tram ticket.

Bike Rentals and Tours

Mountain and road bikes are available from several local shops, including the two best places: **Fitzgerald's Bicycles** (245 W. Hansen St., 307/734-6886, www.fitzgeraldsbicycles.com, 10 A.M.–6 P.M. Mon.–Fri., 10 A.M.–5 P.M. Sat., 10 A.M.–3 P.M. Sun.) and over in Wilson at **Wilson Backcountry Sports** (1230 Ida Dr., 307/733-5228, www.wilsonbackcountry.com). Both of these are full-service pro shops with high-quality full-suspension mountain bikes. Fitzgerald's will even deliver bikes directly to your hotel.

Other area bike shops include:

- **Hoback Sports** (520 W. Broadway Ave., 307/733-5335, www.hobacksports.com)
- **The Edge Sports** (490 W. Broadway Ave., 307/734-3916, www.jacksonholeedgesports.com)
- **Grand Targhee Ski Resort** (in Alta, 307/353-2300 or 800/827-4433, www.grandtarghee.com)
- **Adventure Sports** (307/733-3307, www.dornans.com) in Moose

There are also three Teton Village shops: **Jackson Hole Sports** (307/739-2687, www.jacksonhole.com), **Teton Village Sports** (307/733-2181 or 800/874-4224, www.tetonvillagesports.com), and **Wildernest Sports** (307/733-4297, www.wildernestsports.com). All of these rent standard or cruiser bikes with helmets for $25–42 per day, $15–25 per half-day, and some also have bike trailers, full-suspension mountain bikes, road bikes, hybrid bikes, child bikes, and car racks.

Half-day mountain-bike tours are available from **Fat Tire Tours/Hoback Sports** (307/733-5335, www.hobacksports.com). Options include an easy National Elk Refuge ride ($55) and a more adventurous one ($85) that includes a chairlift ride to the top of Snow King leading into nearby trails. **Teton Mountain Bike Tours** (307/733-0712 or 800/733-0788, www.wybike.com) has scenic half- or all-day bike trips through Grand Teton National Park, Bridger-Teton National Forest, Yellowstone National Park, and the National Elk Refuge. These trips are for all levels of ability, starting at $60 for a four-hour ride in the Antelope Flats area.

ALPINE FUN
Jackson Hole Resort

Take a fast and scenic nine-minute ride to the top of Rendezvous Mountain (10,450 feet) aboard the 100-passenger **aerial tram** (307/733-2292 or 888/333-7766, www.jacksonhole.com, daily 9 A.M.–6 P.M. late May–Sept., $25 adults, $20 seniors, $19 ages 13–17, $12 ages 6–12, free ages five and under) at Teton Village. The tram ride gains more than 4,000 feet in elevation—this is a sensational way to reach the alpine. On top is a small snack shop in Corbet's Cabin with made-to-order waffles and cocoa; bring a lunch if you need something more substantial. Several trails provide enjoyable hikes from the summit, but be sure to pack drinking water and a warm jacket. Dogs and bikes aren't allowed on the tram.

TRAM I AM

For four decades, the main attraction at Jackson Hole Resort was the 52-passenger aerial tram that climbed the summit of Rendezvous Mountain, providing jaw-dropping views across Jackson Hole. But all things must pass. In 2005, Jackson Hole Resort stunned local residents – and skiers around the country – by announcing that the aerial tram would be retired at the end of summer 2006. In operation since 1966, the tram had simply become too worn out to repair. The old one was demolished the following year, and work began on a new and much-improved tram. Opening day for the new $30 million tram came in 2008, much to the relief of skiers, boarders, and Jackson Hole businesses.

Manufactured in Switzerland and powered by 1,970-horsepower engines, the new fire-engine red tram holds 100 people – almost twice the capacity of the old one – and takes nine minutes to get to the summit (versus 12 minutes for the old tram). It can carry 600 passengers per hour, more than twice as many as before.

© DON PITCHER

tram at Jackson Hole Mountain Resort

Rendezvous Mountain is a favorite place for paragliders to launch. Tandem paragliding flights ($245) are available from **Jackson Hole Paragliding** (307/690-8726, www.jhparagliding.com). No experience is needed for these half-hour flights, accessed via the tram.

Summer visitors can also ride the *free* **Bridger gondola** (from 4:30–9 P.M.) to the 9,095-foot level. It doesn't reach the top of the mountain, but affords panoramic vistas over Jackson Hole with access to hiking trails and meals at The Deck and Couloir Restaurant.

Take mountain bikes up the **Teewinot chairlift** (mid-June–early Sept., $10 adults, $8 ages 13–17, $6 ages 6–12, free for younger kids), with seven miles of bike trails on the lower sections of the mountain.

In addition to alpine rides, Teton Village is home to a number of other summer activities on the **Village Commons** ($12 per ticket or $50 for five tickets), including a bungee trampoline and a 25-foot outdoor climbing wall. The big central plaza features a delightful pop-jet fountain, playground, and fire pit, plus an amphitheater for concerts, Teton Raptor Center demonstrations, and storytelling on summer evenings at 5 P.M. Horseback rides, bike rentals, and disc golf are nearby, and child care is available at Kids Ranch (307/739-2654). Stop by the Activity Center for a map and details on all the Teton Village options.

Snow King

At Snow King Mountain right on the edge of Jackson, the resort's main **chairlift** (400 E. Snow King Ave., 307/733-5200 or 800/522-5464, www.snowking.com, daily 9 A.M.–8 P.M. late May–early Sept., $12 adults, $8 ages 7–13, free for kids under 7) takes folks for a 20-minute ride to the summit of the 7,751-foot mountain. On top you'll find a short nature trail, panoramic views of the Tetons, and a myriad of longer hiking and biking trails. Rent a bike at the base of the mountain for a fun ride down.

Also at Snow King is the 2,500-foot-long **Alpine Slide** (307/733-7680 or 800/522-5464, www.snowkingmountain.com), a summertime family favorite. For anyone older than six, the

cost is $15 for one ride or $65 for five rides. For children ages 2–6 riding with an adult it's an additional $3 per ride.

Grand Targhee Ski Resort

On the other side of the Tetons at Grand Targhee Ski Resort (in Alta, 307/353-2300 or 800/827-4433, www.grandtarghee.com), you can ride the **chairlift** ($15 adults, $6 kids) to the 10,200-foot summit of Fred's Mountain, where Grand Teton stands just seven miles away. The lift operates daily late June–mid-September. Mountain bikers can bring a bike (or rent one) to ride the trails high up the slopes; the cost is $20 for an unlimited number of chairlift rides.

SWIMMING AND GYMS

Jackson is home to **Teton County/Jackson Recreation Center** (155 E. Gill St., 307/739-9025, www.tetonwyo.org/parks, 6 A.M.–9 P.M. Mon.–Fri., noon–9 P.M. Sat., noon–7 P.M. Sun.), which includes an indoor aquatics complex with a lap pool, 185-foot corkscrew water slide, and hot tub, plus a wading pool featuring a waterfall, slide, and water geyser. Basketball and volleyball courts are also inside the rec center, and after your workout, relax in the sauna and steam room. Nonresident prices are $7 adults, $5.50 ages 13–17, $4.50 seniors and ages 3–12, and $23 families; free for tots under three. The rec center also offers a variety of courses and activities, including yoga, toddler swimming, basketball, volleyball, and aerobics.

Out of the way is the wonderful hot mineral pool at **Granite Hot Springs** (307/734-7400, http://granitehotsprings.mountainmancountry.com, $6), 35 miles southeast of Jackson. The springs are open daily summer and winter.

Near the Aspens south of Teton Village, **Teton Sports Club** (4030 W. Lake Creek Dr., 307/733-7004, www.tetonsportsclub.com) offers aerobic classes, cardio machines, free weights, indoor and outdoor hot tubs, a sauna, and a summer-only outdoor pool. Day passes are $15. Massage therapists and personal trainers are available.

Jackson Hole Health & Fitness (838 W. Broadway Ave., 307/734-9000, www.jh-healthandfitness.com) houses a state-of-the-art center with machines, weights, bikes, treadmills, elliptical trainers with iPod connectivity, and flat-screen TVs. Day passes are $10.

SPAS

Jackson is a wonderful place to pamper yourself. Most of the top-end hotels provide spa facilities open to both guests and the general public, including Amangani, Rusty Parrot, Snow King Resort, Spring Creek Ranch, Snake River Lodge, Teton Mountain Lodge, Four Seasons Resort, and Hotel Terra. The visitor center has brochures from additional spas, acupuncture clinics, and yoga studios to center your soul. There's even a **Teton Wellness Festival** in early October to get in touch with your inner self (and outer self at the same time). Visit www.tetonwellness.org for links to local centers, from homeopaths to Pilates classes.

ROCK CLIMBING

Jackson Hole is home for two highly regarded climbing schools: **Jackson Hole Mountain Guides** (165 N. Glenwood St., 307/733-4979 or 800/239-7642, www.jhmg.com) and **Exum Mountain Guides** (307/733-2297, www.exumguides.com), with a summertime office at the south end of Jenny Lake. Both offer a wide range of classes—including those for kids and families—plus guided climbs up Grand Teton and wintertime courses in avalanche safety and ice climbing.

Largest indoor rock gym in the Rockies, **Enclosure Indoor Climbing Center** (670 Deer Lane, 307/734-9590, www.enclosureclimbing.com) has a huge diversity of climbing terrain, roped climbing areas, and bouldering, plus a fitness center and even child care. There's also an outdoor climbing wall in Teton Village and at Grand Targhee Resort.

AERIAL RIDES

Two local companies offer early morning hot-air balloon rides in the summer: **Wyoming Balloon Co.** (307/739-0900, www.wyomingballoon.com) and **Endeavor Ballooning** (307/699-1339, www.wyoming-hotair.com). Adult rates are $295 per person for these hour-long flights.

The top of the Jackson Hole Resort tram is a favorite place for paragliders to launch. Tandem paragliding flights ($225) are available from **Jackson Hole Paragliding** (307/739-2626, www.jhparagliding.com). No experience is needed for these 15-minute flights.

Cowboy Up Hang Gliding (307/413-4164, www.cuhanggliding.com) has tandem flights from Alpine (35 miles southwest of Jackson), using an ultralight to gain altitude for flights over the Salt River Range. These cost $169 for a flight that lasts at least 20 minutes.

Over the pass in Driggs, Idaho, **Teton Aviation Center** (208/354-3100 or 800/472-6382, www.tetonaviation.com) has glider flights,at $250 for a one-hour flight; they're a great way to come eye-to-eye with Grand Teton.

GOLF AND TENNIS

Like many resort areas, Jackson Hole has an abundance of tony golf courses, including five in the valley plus another six over the pass in Teton Valley. **Jackson Hole Golf and Tennis Club** (307/733-3111, www.jhgtc.com), one mile north of town, has a public 18-hole golf course designed by Robert Trent Jones Jr. and rated one of the 10 best in America. Also here are a private swimming pool, tennis courts, fitness center, and North Grille Restaurant (11:30 A.M.–close in summer) for patio dining.

Teton Pines Country Club (on Teton Village Rd., 307/733-1773 or 800/238-2223, www.tetonpines.com) is Jackson Hole's other golf spot open to the public. Its Arnold Palmer–designed 18-hole championship course is very challenging; 14 of the holes require over-water shots. The club also features a grand clubhouse, tennis courts, and a large (and private) outdoor pool, along with fine dining at The Pines restaurant. Both Teton Pines and Jackson Hole Golf and Tennis Club have rentals and lessons for golfers and tennis aficionados.

The Tom Fazio–designed 18-hole course **Shooting Star Golf Course** (307/739-3260 or 877/739-8062, www.shootingstarjh.com) opened in 2009 next to Teton Village. It is, however, only for members, and at $100,000 per, it's a bit beyond the range of most mortals!

For the dedicated miniature golfer, **Alpine Miniature Golf** (307/733-5200 or 800/522-5464, www.snowking.com, $8) has a Lilliputian 18-hole hillside course next to the Alpine Slide at Snow King Resort.

Public tennis courts are on the east end of the rodeo grounds along Snow King Drive, and within Miller Park at Deloney and Gill Streets.

TOWN PARKS

Eight parks are scattered around Jackson, including the famous Town Square. Several others are of note, particularly if you have children in tow. The largest, **Miller Park,** covers a grassy city block at Deloney and Gill Streets and includes basketball and tennis courts, a picnic shelter, restrooms, and a delightful playground. **Powderhorn Park,** on the west side of town near Powderhorn and Alpine Lanes, has additional playground equipment, a picnic shelter, and restrooms. **Mike Yokel Jr. Park,** on East Kelly Avenue near Snow King, features a sand volleyball court, horseshoe pits, a playground, a picnic shelter, and restrooms. **Baux Park** at the base of Snow King Mountain is similar, with a playground, horseshoe pits, and picnic tables. **Home Ranch Park** is next to the parking lot at Cache and Gill and has picnic tables and restrooms. **Owen Bircher Park** in Wilson includes a summertime roping arena (a good place to watch budding cowboys and cowgirls on summer afternoons) that becomes a wintertime ice rink. The park also has a sand volleyball court, a softball/soccer field, picnic tables, and restrooms.

In addition to those mentioned in the town parks, public restrooms can be found half a block south of Town Square on Cache Drive.

Winter Recreation

Jackson Hole has an international reputation as a winter destination. As access has become easier and the facilities more developed, many people have discovered the wonders of a Jackson Hole winter, especially one centered on a week of skiing or snowboarding. Three very different ski resorts attract the crowds: Grand Targhee for down-home, powder-to-the-butt conditions; Snow King for steep, inexpensive, edge-of-town slopes; and Jackson Hole for flashy, world-class skiing. All three places have rental equipment, ski schools, and special programs for kids. Snowboarders and telemarkers are welcome on the slopes. These resorts combine with an incredible abundance of developed and wild places to ski cross-country to make Jackson Hole one of the premier ski and snowboard destinations in America.

See a travel agent for package trips to any of the Jackson-area resorts. For daily ski reports, including information on both downhill and Nordic areas and the backcountry, listen to KMTN (FM 96.9) in the morning or visit resort websites. Both Jackson Hole Resort and Grand Targhee also post snow updates on Twitter.

DOWNHILL SKIING AND SNOWBOARDING

If you plan to spend more than a couple of days in the area, it is probably worth your while to join the **Jackson Hole Ski and Snowboard Club** (307/733-6433, www.jhskiclub.com). In return for a $30 membership, you receive an impressive number of premiums, including reduced rates for lift tickets and season passes, plus discounted lodging, meals, drinks, snowmobile trips, and shopping at local stores. Join online or at their office inside Snow King Resort (400 E. Snow King Ave.).

Grand Targhee Ski Resort (307/353-2300 or 800/827-4433, www.grandtarghee.com)— just five miles above Alta, Wyoming—is the main attraction for the Teton Valley, Idaho area. The resort offers excellent skiing and snowboarding in winter, along with a wide range of summer activities.

Ski and Snowboard Rentals

Rent or buy downhill skis and snowboards from **Hoback Sports** (520 W. Broadway Ave., 307/733-5335, www.hobacksports. com), **Boardroom of Jackson Hole** (225 W. Broadway Ave., 307/733-8327, www.boardroomjacksonhole.com), **The Edge Sports** (490 W. Broadway Ave., 307/734-3916, www.jacksonholeedgesports.com), **Gart Sports** (485 W. Broadway Ave., 307/733-4449, www.gartsports.com), **Jack Dennis Sports** (50 E. Broadway Ave., 307/733-3270 or 800/570-3270, www.jackdennisoutdoors.com; and in Teton Village, 307/733-6838), **Jackson Hole Sports** (in Teton Village, 307/739-2687, www.jacksonhole.com), **Pepi Stiegler Sports** (in Teton Village, 307/733-4505, www.pepistieglers.com), **Wildernest Sports** (in Teton Village, 307/733-4297, www.wildernestsports.com), or **Teton Village Sports** (307/733-2181 or 800/874-4224, www.tetonvillagesports.com). Rentals are also available at all three ski areas.

◖ Jackson Hole Mountain Resort

Just 12 miles northwest of Jackson is Jackson Hole Mountain Resort (307/733-2292 or 888/333-7766, www.jacksonhole.com), the largest and best-known Wyoming ski area. A true skiers' and snowboarders' mountain, Jackson Hole is considered the most varied and challenging of any American ski area. The powder is usually deep (average annual snowfall is 38 feet), lift lines are short, the slopes are relatively uncrowded, and the vistas are unbelievable. First opened in 1965, Jackson Hole Mountain Resort has become one of the nation's favorite ski areas. The resort has invested many millions of dollars in the last decade or so, upgrading facilities, adding lifts,

expanding snowmaking, completing a spacious children's center, and building an ice rink and snowboarding half-pipe. These improvements have both enhanced the resort's reputation as an expert's paradise and added facilities that are friendlier to families and intermediate skiers. Jackson Hole Mountain Resort is owned by the Kemmerer family, whose ancestors founded the town of Kemmerer, Wyoming, and is one of the few major American ski resorts that is still independently owned. The resort is trying to become eco-friendly; it gets all its energy from renewable energy credits and recycling a third of all trash.

The mountain has one unusual feature that occurs in midwinter: A temperature inversion frequently develops over the valley, meaning that when it's bitterly cold at the base of the mountain, the top is 15–20°F warmer. Skiers often remain on the upper slopes all day to enjoy these warmer temperatures.

With an unsurpassed 4,139-foot vertical drop (longest in the United States), 2,500 acres of terrain spread over two adjacent mountains, runs that exceed four miles in length, and 24 miles of groomed trails, Jackson Hole Mountain Resort is truly a place of superlatives. Half of the resort's 60 runs are in the advanced category—including several of the notorious double-diamonds—but it is so large that even beginners will find plenty of bunny slopes on which to practice. (As a trivial aside, Montana's Big Sky Resort also claims the longest vertical drop of any American mountain—4,300 feet—but this involves taking three lifts and ending your run below where you start.)

The only way to the summit of 10,450-foot **Rendezvous Mountain** is aboard one of the 100-passenger aerial tram cars. Powered by 1,970-horsepower engines, they climb nearly 2.5 miles in nine minutes, offering jaw-dropping views across Jackson Hole. Rendezvous Mountain is where experts strut their stuff on these steep and fast slopes, and if you're not at least close to expert status you'll find your blood pressure rising as the tram heads up the mountain. More than a few skiers and boarders have taken the tram back down after seeing what lies below. Yes, those death-defying cliff-jumping shots are real; check out infamous **Corbet's Couloir,** a rocky gully that requires a leap of faith. Fortunately, intermediate skiers and boarders are not given short shrift at Jackson Hole Mountain Resort, particularly on the friendlier slopes of 8,481-foot **Après Vous Mountain.** Intermediate (and advanced) downhillers could spend all day playing on these slopes, and a high-speed quad here means that riders can blast to the summit of Après Vous in just five minutes. Because of the speed of this and other lifts, the wait at the base is usually just a few minutes.

In addition to these lifts, you can ride a gondola, five other quad chairs, two triple chairs, a double chair, and a Poma lift. Snowboarders will appreciate the half-pipe and boarders' terrain trail. The resort's **Kids Ranch** (307/739-2788, $89 per day) provides supervised day care, including a spacious play area; it's the only drop-off day-care center in Jackson Hole, and it's open seven days a week in winter. Not far away is a special "magic carpet" (a conveyer belt of sorts) for children learning to ski or snowboard.

Summer visitors to Jackson Hole Mountain Resort find an amazing variety of activities including horseback rides, music festivals, rock-climbing, paragliding, a mountain biking course, disc golf, playful pop-jet fountains, a bungee trampoline, shopping, or just soaking up the view while nursing a beer.

RATES AND SERVICES

Get to Teton Village from the town of Jackson by hopping on the START bus ($3 each way; 307/733-4521, www.startbus.com). This is the only inexpensive part of a visit to Jackson Hole Resort, where prices for lift tickets approach the stratosphere. Regular-season single-day tickets are $91 adults, $55 ages 6–14, and $68 seniors. Afternoon-only rates are $73 adults, $44 kids, and $55 seniors. Multi-day tickets—the most common kind bought—are $435 per week (five days of skiing) for adults, $260 for kids 5–14, and $325 for seniors. Lifts are open 9 A.M.–4 P.M. daily Thanksgiving–early April.

Skis and snowboards can be rented at shops in Jackson or Teton Village. The ski school offers a Kids Ranch program with age-specific skiing and boarding. Jackson Hole Resort even has special steep snowboarding and skiing camps, where you learn from extreme downhill fanatics. Tommy Moe—gold and silver medalist at the 1994 Winter Olympics—is a ski ambassador for the resort. A private day of guided skiing is available for $1,400 (intermediate and expert skiers only).

Ski hosts provide information and twice-daily tours from the front of Walk Festival Hall. Racers and spectators will enjoy NASTAR events, along with various other competitions throughout the winter.

Get recorded snow conditions by calling the **Snowphone** at 307/733-2291; messages are changed each morning before 5 A.M. The resort's website is packed with additional details, including the current weather and snow conditions, or visit www.jacksonhole.com/mobile from your iPhone.

Into the Backcountry

If you're looking for untracked powder, the Jackson Hole Mountain Resort (307/733-2292 or 888/333-7766, www.jacksonhole.com) can set up private lessons for access to parts of the mountain that are off-limits to mere mortals.

In lower Rock Springs Canyon, two miles south of the resort, **Rock Springs Yurt** has a backcountry location that's accessible by cross-country skis or snowshoes. It's only a two-mile trek, but you gain 1,000 feet along the way, making this a challenging trip. The fully equipped yurt is available for guided day trips and overnight stays. It sleeps eight for $425, including dinner and breakfast cooked by the "yurt meister." Contact Jackson Hole Resort (307/739-2663 or 800/450-0477, www.jacksonhole.com) for details. The yurt is also open to summertime hikers.

Powderhound skiers with a ton of cash will find unparalleled outback conditions accessible via **High Mountain Heli-Skiing** (307/733-3274, www.heliskijackson.com). Operating from Togwotee Mountain Lodge (307/543-

2847 or 800/543-2847, www.togwoteelodge. com) 48 miles northeast of Jackson, **Togwotee Snowcat Skiing** takes skiers and snowboarders into a wide variety of terrain with spectacular vistas of the Tetons en route.

Teton Village

At the base of Rendezvous Mountain is the Swiss-style Teton Village—alias "the Vill." Everything skiers and boarders need is crowded together here: lodges, condominiums, espresso stands, restaurants, après-ski bars, gift shops, groceries, ski, snowboard, and snowshoe rentals and lessons, storage lockers, car rentals, a sledding hill, child care, personal trainers, dogsled tours, and even a travel agency for escapes to Hawaii. Tune your radio to FM 100.1 "Teton Village Radio" for parking and transportation information.

On-the-mountain facilities include a fine-dining establishment (Couloir Restaurant) at the top of Bridger gondola, Casper Restaurant at the bottom of Casper Bowl, and snack bars at the base of Thunder chairlift and the top of Après Vous chairlift. Casper Restaurant serves a barbecue picnic most days and is a popular place to join friends for lunch.

Snow King Mountain

Snow King Mountain (307/734-3136, www. snowkingmountain.com) has three things that other local ski areas lack: location, location, and location. The resort sits directly behind town and just seven blocks from Town Square. This is the locals' place, Jackson's "town hill," but it also offers surprisingly challenging runs. It may not be the largest or fanciest place around, but the King's ski runs make up in difficulty what they lack in size. From below, the mountain (7,808 feet at the summit) looks impossibly steep and narrow. High atop the big chairlift, the vista provides a panoramic tour of Jackson Hole and the Tetons.

Snow King was the first ski area in Wyoming—it opened in 1939—and one of the first in North America. The original chapter of the National Ski Patrol was established here in 1941. The mountain has a 1,571-foot

vertical drop. You'll find more than 400 acres of skiable terrain at Snow King, with the longest run stretching nearly a mile. A triple chair, two double chairs, and a Poma lift climb the mountainside. Other features include snow-making, a tubing park, and a very popular terrain park for snowboarders. It's the only local resort with lighted runs.

RATES AND SERVICES

Prices for lift tickets at Snow King are well below those at other Jackson Hole resorts: $42 per day ($32 per half-day) for adults and $32 per day ($22 per half-day) for kids under 13 and seniors. Hours of operation are daily 10 A.M.–4 P.M., with **night skiing** (4–7 P.M. Tues.–Sat.) available on the lower sections of Snow King for an additional $20 adults or $15 kids and seniors. In addition, the King has special three-hour rates for lift tickets ($30 adults, $20 kids and seniors); these are perfect for skiers and boarders who arrive late in the afternoon and want to hit the slopes for a bit. With some of the best snowmaking in Wyoming, the resort usually opens by Thanksgiving and remains in operation through early April.

At the base of Snow King you'll discover a lodge with reasonable ski-and-stay packages. Also at Snow King are two restaurants, a lounge (called, not surprisingly, The Lounge), ski and snowboard rentals and lessons, plus a variety of other facilities, including an indoor ice rink and mountaintop snack shack. Jackson's START buses (307/733-4521, www. startbus.com) provide frequent service to town (free) or Teton Village ($3).

CROSS-COUNTRY SKIING

For many Jackson Hole residents, the word "skiing" means heading across frozen Jenny Lake or telemarking down the bowls of Teton Pass rather than sliding down the slopes of the local resorts. Jackson Hole has become a center for cross-country enthusiasts and offers an impressive range of conditions—from flat-tracking along summertime golf courses where a gourmet restaurant awaits to remote wilderness settings where a complete knowledge of snowpack structure, avalanche hazards, and winter survival techniques is essential. Beginners will probably want to start out at a Nordic center, progressing to local paths and the more gentle lift-serviced ski runs with experience. More advanced skiers will quickly discover incredible snow in the surrounding mountains.

Ski Rentals

Rent or buy cross-country skis from **Skinny Skis** (65 W. Deloney Ave., 307/733-6094 or 888/733-7205, www.skinnyskis.com), **Teton Mountaineering** (170 N. Cache Dr., 307/733-3595 or 800/850-3595, www.tetonmtn.com), or **Wilson Backcountry Sports** (Wilson, 307/733-5228, www.wilsonbackcountry.com). Local Nordic centers also rent equipment. Most places rent both classical cross-country skis and skate skis (much faster and a better workout), along with telemark and alpine touring skis.

Nordic Centers

Nordic skiing enthusiasts will find two different developed facilities near Jackson and a third at Grand Targhee in Alta, Wyoming. The largest is **Jackson Hole Nordic Center** (307/739-2629, www.jacksonhole.com) in Teton Village, with 15 kilometers of groomed trails—both set track and skating lanes—that cover a wide range of conditions. Call 307/733-2291 for the snow report. This is the best place to learn cross-country skiing. Daily trail passes are $14. Traditional cross-country skis, skate skis, and telemarking equipment are available for rent, and the center offers a wide spectrum of lessons and tours. Hours are daily 8:30 A.M.–4:30 P.M. You can exchange your alpine lift ticket at Jackson Hole Mountain Resort for one at the Nordic center (but, hey, it had better be for no extra charge since you've already dropped $91!).

Along Teton Village Road, **Teton Pines** (307/733-1005 or 800/238-2223, www.tetonpines.com) features 16 kilometers of immaculately groomed track (both classical and skating) on a summertime golf course. Daily trail passes cost $10 adults or $5 children and seniors. Ski rentals and lessons are available. Hours are daily 9 A.M.–5 P.M. The clubhouse here has a restaurant for gourmet après-ski lunches and dinners.

On the west side of the Tetons 42 miles out of Jackson, **Grand Targhee Nordic Center** (307/353-2300 or 800/827-4433, www.grandtarghee.com) has 15 kilometers of groomed cross-country ski trails (classical and skating) covering rolling terrain. Trail passes are $10 adults and $6 seniors and kids. Lessons and ski rentals are also available. Hours are daily 9:30 A.M.–4 P.M. Guests with Targhee lodging packages can ski free on the cross-country tracks.

On Your Own

Nordic skiers who would rather explore Jackson Hole and the mountains that surround it on their own will discover an extraordinary range of options, from beginner-level treks along old roads to places where only the most advanced skiers dare venture. Because Jackson has so many cross-country fanatics (and visiting enthusiasts), tracks are quickly broken along the more popular routes, making it easier for those who follow. For complete coverage of all these options, pick up a copy of the helpful free winter outdoors guide *Trailhead* at Skinny Skis (65 W. Deloney Ave., 307/733-6094 or 888/733-7205, www.skinnyskis.com). If you're heading out on your own, be prepared for deep snow (four feet in the valley) and temperatures that often plummet below zero at night.

Teton County Parks & Recreation (155 E. Gill, 307/739-9025, www.tetonwyo.org/parks) leads all-day cross-country ski and snowshoe outings in winter, as well as cross-country lessons. The department also grooms 30 kilometers of local pathways for cross-country and skate skiing in the winter; call 307/739-6789 for the grooming hotline with daily updates. **Friends of Pathways** (307/733-9562, www.friendsofpathways.org) produces a free map of local Nordic trails (including the grooming schedule) and has a downloadable version on their website.

JACKSON AREA

Even beginners will enjoy exploring several local spots. The closest place to Jackson for on-your-own cross-country skiing is **Cache Creek Canyon.** The trailhead is at the east end of Cache Creek Drive, where the plowing ends at a parking lot. The trail is groomed by Parks & Rec a couple of times per week. For a longer trip, take the Rafferty ski lift at Snow King and then ski west through the trees and down to Cache Creek, returning via the road. Ask at Snow King Resort (400 E. Snow King Ave., 307/733-5200 or 800/522-5464, www.snowking.com) for specifics and safety precautions.

Another popular local place is along the **Snake River dikes,** where Highway 22 crosses the river one mile east of Wilson. The dikes extend along both sides of the river for several miles, making for easy skiing. This is also a good place to watch ducks, moose, and other critters or to listen to the river rolling over the rocks. The northeast side is groomed for skate and touring skis on a regular basis but can get pockmarked by folks walking the trail.

GRANITE HOT SPRINGS

One of the most popular ski- and snowmobile-in sites is Granite Hot Springs (307/734-7400, http://granitehotsprings.mountainmancountry.com), a delightful hot spring–fed pool on Forest Service land. Get there by driving 25 miles southeast of Jackson into Hoback Canyon and then skiing 10 miles in from the signed parking area. The route is not difficult, but because of the distance it isn't recommended for beginners unless they're prepared for a 20-mile round-trip trek. The pool costs $6 adults, $4 ages 3–12, and is free for infants. It's open daily 10 A.M.–5 P.M. in winter. Bring your swimsuit or rent a suit and towel here. Ask the attendant about places to snow camp nearby.

TETON PASS

Locals head to 8,429-foot Teton Pass when they really want to test their abilities. The summit parking area fills with cars on fresh-snow mornings as everyone from advanced beginners to world-class ski mountaineers heads out for a day in the powder or a week of wilderness trekking in the Tetons. Snow depths of eight feet or more are not uncommon in midwinter. (The snow once became so deep on the pass that it took plows two weeks to clear the road!) The slopes around Teton Pass cover the full spectrum, but be sure you know your own ability and how to avoid avalanches. Check the previously mentioned Skinny Skis *Trailhead* winter guide for specifics on Teton Pass, or talk to folks at Skinny Skis or Teton Mountaineering. This is the backcountry, so you won't see any signs at the various bowls; ask other skiers if you aren't sure which is which. Avalanches do occur in some of these bowls, and it's possible to get lost up here during a storm, so come prepared.

Those without backcountry experience should contact **Rendezvous Backcountry Tours** (307/353-2900 or 877/754-4887, www.skithetetons.com), **Jackson Hole Mountain Guides** (307/733-4979 or 800/239-7642, www.jhmg.com), **Exum Mountain Guides** (307/733-2297, www.exumguides.com), or **Jackson Hole Nordic Center** (307/739-2629, www.jacksonhole.com) for guided ski tours at Teton Pass and elsewhere.

Ski Tours

Both **Jackson Hole Mountain Guides** (307/733-4979 or 800/239-7642, www.jhmg.com) and **Exum Mountain Guides** (307/733-2297, www.exumguides.com) run winter ascents of Grand Teton, plus avalanche safety courses and ski mountaineering trips. Longer winter trips, including a five-day Teton Crest tour, are also available.

Over on the western slopes of the Tetons, **Rendezvous Backcountry Tours** (307/353-2900 or 877/754-4887, www.skithetetons.com) maintains three Mongolian-style yurts in the Jedediah Smith Wilderness, each situated several hours of skiing (or hiking) from the next. These immensely popular huts can sleep up to eight and have kitchens, bunks, sleeping bags, and woodstoves; they're $375 per night on weekends ($325 on weekdays) plus $150 for a guide to take you in on the first day. You'll need to be experienced in backcountry skiing and have the necessary safety equipment and avalanche training. If you don't quite measure up, the company provides guided ski tours to the huts. A three-day, two-night catered trip is $695 per person including guide, porter service, meals, lodging, sleeping bags, and avalanche equipment. The backcountry yurts are available December–April, but call far ahead for reservations. The most popular one (Baldy Knoll) fills a year in advance! Rendezvous also has a close-in family yurt ($95 d or $150 for up to six guests). It's open year-round, with drive-up access in summer and a 0.5-mile walk in winter. The family hut has running water, a kitchen, and bath, while the backcountry yurts have outhouses.

Jackson Hole Nordic Center (307/739-2629, www.jacksonhole.com), at Teton Village, has guided ski tours into Grand Teton National Park; a half-day for two people costs $160.

ICE-SKATING

Each winter, the town of Wilson floods the town park for skating, hockey, and broomball. A warming hut stands next to the rink. In Jackson, the rodeo arena at the fairgrounds (552 S. Snow King Ave.) becomes a winter ice rink for broomball and open skating. Both rinks are free and lighted most winter evenings. Contact Teton County Parks & Recreation (307/733-5056, www.tetonwyo.org/parks) for details.

For the out-of-the-elements version, skate over to **Snow King Resort** (400 E. Snow King Ave., 307/733-5200 or 800/522-5464, www.snowking.com), where the indoor ice-skating rink is open in the winter and offers skate rentals and lessons. In addition, **Grand Targhee Ski Resort** (in Alta, 307/353-2300 or 800/827-4433, www.grandtarghee.com) has a skating pond with rentals.

SNOWSHOEING

Snowshoeing began as a way to get around in the winter, but the old-fashioned wood-and-rawhide snowshoes were bulky and heavy. In recent years snowshoeing has become a popular form of recreation, as new technology created lightweight and easily maneuverable snowshoes. Snowshoeing requires no real training: Just strap the snowshoes on, grab a pair of poles, and start walking. But be careful where you walk.

Rent snowshoes from **Skinny Skis** (65 W. Deloney Ave., 307/733-6094 or 888/733-7205, www.skinnyskis.com), **Teton Mountaineering** (170 N. Cache Dr., 307/733-3595 or 800/850-3595, www.tetonmtn.com), **Wilson Backcountry Sports** (in Wilson, 307/733-5228, www.wilsonbackcountry.com), or **Grand Targhee Ski Resort** (in Alta, 307/353-2300 or 800/827-4433, www.grandtarghee.com).

Guided Trips

Teton County Parks & Recreation (155 E. Gill, 307/739-9025, www.tetonwyo.org/parks) leads snowshoe tours periodically throughout the winter. Snowshoe walks into the mountains around Jackson are also offered by **The Hole Hiking Experience** (307/690-4453 or 866/733-4453, www.holehike.com), the only company permitted to guide snowshoeing trips in nearby national forests. Their most popular trips go to Shadow Mountain north of Kelly. Rates start at $95 adults, $75 kids for a four-hour snowshoe trek (minimum of three people).

Also check out A. J. DeRosa's **Wildlife Snowshoe Adventures** (307/732-2628, www.woodboattours.com), combining snowshoe hikes with lunch or dinner at a riverside teepee.

The Saddlehorn Activity Center at **Jackson Hole Mountain Resort** (307/733-2292 or 888/333-7766, www.jacksonhole.com) has snowshoe rentals and tours. In addition, a snowshoe trail parallels Nordic Center ski tracks, and Forest Service naturalists lead snowshoe hikes in the area on Wednesday and Saturday.

Free naturalist-led snowshoe tours are offered at **Grand Targhee Ski Resort** (in Alta, 307/353-2300 or 800/827-4433, www.grandtarghee.com). Additionally, naturalist-led snowshoe hikes are available in Grand Teton National Park.

SLEIGH RIDES

Several companies offer romantic dinner and horse-drawn sleigh rides in the Jackson Hole area mid-December–March. Make reservations well in advance for these popular trips. If you don't have the cash for one of these, take a daytime sleigh ride at the National Elk Refuge.

Jackson Hole Mountain Resort (307/733-2674, www.tetonvillagetrailrides.com, $80 adults, $70 children under 11, and free for infants) picks up Teton Village guests for a romantic 30-minute ride to Cascade Restaurant at Teton Mountain Lodge, where they are offered a variety of dinner options. Reservations are recommended. If you're just looking for a Teton Village sleigh ride, there is a 12-person sleigh ($35 adults, $25 kids) or a private ride on a romantic "Cinderella" sleigh ($100 for up to four people). Both options last approximately 30–40 minutes.

Spring Creek Ranch (307/733-8833 or 800/443-6139, www.springcreekranch.com) has 45-minute afternoon sleigh rides ($39 per person) at the top of Gros Ventre Butte. It also has packages ($89 per person for adults, $59 kids) that combine a sleigh ride with a meal at the Granary Restaurant. This is one of Jackson's finer restaurants, so bring your dress clothes and make reservations.

Mill Iron Ranch (307/733-6390 or 888/808-6390, www.millironranch.net, $85 adults, $60 kids) is a friendly family-run operation with evening sleigh rides in a down-home setting 10 miles south of Jackson in Horse Creek Canyon. Guests get a 45-minute ride that takes them past an elk herd to the lodge for a big T-bone steak dinner. In scenic Horse Creek Canyon, this is the most authentic of the local sleigh rides. Call for reservations.

Dinner sleigh rides are also offered at **Grand Targhee Ski Resort** (in Alta, 307/353-2300 or 800/827-4433, www.grandtarghee.com, $40 adults, $15 kids), where a horse-drawn sleigh transports you to a remote yurt for a Western-style meal.

TUBING

Two local ski areas have sliding parks with customized inner tubes and rope tows. At Snow King Resort the park is called **King Tubes** (307/734-8823 or 800/522-5464, www.jacksonholesnowtubing.com) and is available on weekday evenings and weekends after noon. Rates are $16 for one hour or $21 for two hours for adults; $13 for one hour or $18 for two hours for kids. The **Grand Targhee tube park** (307/353-2300 or 800/827-4433, www.grandtarghee.com) is open for après-ski fun only (after 5 P.M.) and costs $10.

DOGSLEDDING

Founded by eight-time Iditarod musher Frank Teasley, **Jackson Hole Iditarod Sled Dog Tours** (307/733-7388 or 800/554-7388, www.jhsleddog.com) has excellent half-day ($225 per person including lunch) and all-day trips ($295 per person including a big steak or trout dinner). The main destination is wonderful Granite Hot Springs (accessible only on all-day rides), but when snow conditions are right, the teams may run in the Cliff Creek, Grays River, Shadow Mountain, and Gros Ventre areas. All trips include round-trip transportation from Jackson to his base on the Hoback River.

Another Iditarod veteran, Billy Snodgrass, operates **Continental Divide Dogsled Adventures** (307/739-0165 or 800/531-6874, www.dogsledadventures.com), with dog teams at Togwotee Mountain Lodge (48 miles north of Jackson). Half-day tours in this gorgeous country are $224 per person, including lunch and transportation from Jackson. All-day tours are $270 and longer trips are also available, including a two-day adventure in which you stay overnight in a backcountry yurt or at luxurious Brooks Lake Lodge.

SNOWMOBILING

Snowmobiling is one of Jackson Hole's most popular wintertime activities. Hundreds of miles of packed and groomed snowmobile trails head into Bridger-Teton National Forest. Some of the most popular places include the Togwotee Pass area 48 miles north of Jackson,

Cache Creek Road east of town, and Granite Hot Springs Road 25 miles southeast. Only guided snowmobile groups are allowed into Yellowstone, with all-day tours to Old Faithful ($270 for one rider or $390 for two riders).

Tours to other areas are usually less expensive, and some motels offer package deals. The visitor center has brochures and a complete listing of local snowmobile-rental companies, plus maps of snowmobile trails.

Entertainment and Events

Jackson Hole has a wide range of entertainment options: cowboy bars where saddles double as bar stools, classical concerts beneath the stars, playful family musicals, rodeos and chuck-wagon dinners, and much more.

At the modern 525-seat theater within **Jackson Hole Center for the Arts** (307/733-4900, www.jhcenterforthearts.org) you might see everyone from Leo Kottke and Herbie Hancock to the Preservation Hall Jazz Band and Willie Nelson.

In 2009, Teton County instituted a no-smoking measure that prohibits smoking in restaurants, bars, and workplaces, along with many outdoor locations such as chairlift lines, restaurant patios, and sports arenas. Because of this, virtually all Jackson Hole restaurants and bars are now entirely smoke-free. The only exception is the smoky Virginian Bar (750 W. Broadway Ave.) on the south end of town. (This will change if the Virginian loses an ongoing lawsuit over the issue.) Jackson Hole Mountain Resort, Grand Targhee Resort, and Snow King Resort all prohibit smoking except in designated areas.

NIGHTLIFE

Barflies will keep buzzing in Jackson, especially during midsummer and midwinter, when visitors pack local saloons every night of the week. At least one club always seems to have live tunes; check Jackson's free newspapers to see what's where. Cover charges are generally $5 on the weekends, and most other times you'll get in free. See the free *Jackson Hole Weekly* (307/732-0299, www.planetjh.com) for upcoming music and other entertainment.

The famous **Million Dollar Cowboy Bar** (on the west side of Town Square, 307/733-2207, www.milliondollarcowboybar.com) is a favorite of real cowboys and their wannabe cousins. Inside the Cowboy you'll discover burled lodgepole pine beams, four pool tables (nearly always in use), display cases with stuffed dead bears and other cuddly critters, bars inlaid with old silver dollars, and bar stools made from old saddles. Until the 1950s, the Cowboy was Jackson's center for illegal gambling. Bartenders kept a close eye on Teton Pass, where messengers used mirrors to deliver warnings of coming federal revenuers, giving folks at the bar time to hide the gaming tables in a back room. Today the dance floor fills with honky-tonking couples as the bands croon lonesome cowboy tunes six nights a week (Mon.–Sat.). Looking to learn swing and two-step dancing? You can join an excellent free beginners' class at 7:30 P.M. every Thursday, and then dance up a storm when the band comes on at 9.

Silver Dollar Bar & Grill (50 N. Glenwood St., 307/732-3939, www.worthotel.com) inside the Wort Hotel offers a setting that might seem more fitting in Las Vegas: Gaudy pink neon lights curve around a bar inlaid with 2,032 (count 'em!) silver dollars. It tends to attract an older crowd with nightly drink specials (best martinis in Jackson), but Tuesday nights are the notable exception, when bluegrass bands and no cover attract a packed house of partying 20-somethings.

In Teton Village is **Mangy Moose Restaurant & Saloon** (307/733-4913, www.mangymoose.net) Jackson Hole's jumpingest pickup spot and *the* place to rock out. The Moose attracts a hip skier/outdoorsy crowd with rock, blues, or world beat bands (Wed.–Sat.,

© DON PITCHER

Jackson's famed Million Dollar Cowboy Bar

sometimes nightly) both summer and winter. This is also where you'll hear nationally known acts. Upcoming acts are listed on the Mangy Moose website. The on-site restaurant serves food until 10 P.M.

On the way to Teton Village, and next door to Calico Restaurant, **Q Roadhouse** (2550 Moose-Wilson Rd., 307/739-0700, www. qjacksonhole.com, daily 5–10 P.M.) is a cavernous, indestructible pub (concrete floors and an industrial décor), where the menu includes wings, blackened catfish, and jambalaya. Toss your peanut shells on the floor and join the happy crowds of locals listening to rock tunes (live bands Thurs. nights) and putting back the beers.

Jammed against the hill on the west end of town, **Sidewinders Sports Grill & Tavern** (802 W. Broadway Ave., 307/734-5766, www. sidewinderstavern.com, daily 11:30 A.M.– 12:30 A.M.) is a bar/restaurant with pub grub, 30 beers on tap, and a couple-dozen flat-screen TVs for sports enthusiasts. Look for the enormous American flag out front. Downstairs is

trendy **Ignight** (307/734-1997, www.ignight-jacksonhole.com, $8–14), with freshly squeezed juice cocktails at the martini bar, along with sushi, ceviche, salads, and a variety of finger food. Live music (Thurs.–Sat. nights) enlivens the classy setting.

The Granary (307/733-8833 or 800/443-6139, www.springcreekranch.com) atop East Gros Ventre Butte has mellow jazz (Fri. nights) and piano tunes (Sat.).

Over in Wilson, **The Stagecoach Bar** (307/733-4407) is *the* place to be on Sunday nights 6–10 P.M., when locals call it "the church." In the 1970s, when hippies risked getting their heads shaved by rednecks at Jackson's Cowboy Bar, they found the 'Coach a more tolerant place. Today, tobacco-chewing cowpokes show their partners slick moves on the tiny dance floor as the Stagecoach Band (jokingly known as the "worst country-western band in the U.S.") runs through the country tunes one more time; the band has performed here every Sunday since 1969! Outside you'll find picnic tables and a volleyball court for pickup games in the summer, or pick up a cue stick and show off your billiard skills indoors. The Mexican-infused bar food comes from Pica's Taqueria, with burritos, tacos, burgers, quesadillas, and more. Also popular are the Thursday-night disco parties with a dance-club atmosphere and a fog machine; it's a great time to dress up in *Saturday Night Fever* garb.

THE ARTS

In addition to the bar scene, summers bring several lighthearted acting ventures to Jackson. For family musicals such as *Paint Your Wagon, Nunsense,* or *Annie Get Your Gun,* head to **Jackson Hole Playhouse** (145 W. Deloney, 307/733-6994, www.jhplayhouse.com). Shows take place Monday–Saturday evenings in a campy 1890s-style setting; tickets are $26 adults, $22 ages 13–18, and $19 ages 5–12. A family saloon (no alcohol; what kind of a saloon is that?) and restaurant are next door. More serious productions are offered in the winter.

A professional repertory group, the **Off Square Theatre Company** (307/733-3670, www.offsquare.org) stages Broadway comedies in the summer at the Jackson Hole Center for the Arts, with dramatic productions the rest of the year.

In existence for more than 50 years, the **Grand Teton Music Festival** (307/733-1128, www.gtmf.org) takes place at Walk Festival Hall in Teton Village, with performances of classical and modern works by a cast of 200 world-renowned symphony musicians. Concerts are at 8 P.M. from the first of July to mid-August each year, with free "Inside the Music" concerts on Tuesday, Wednesday-night spotlight concerts ($41 adults, $10 kids) featuring jazz, bluegrass, and Afro-Cuban music, and Thursday-night "musicians' choice" classical chamber music ($25 adults, $10 kids). Full festival orchestra concerts on Friday and Saturday are $52 adults, $10 kids. They also perform a free outdoor **Music in the Hole** patriotic concert on the Fourth of July for an audience that tops 8,000, plus special youth concerts and other events. Three-hour-long Friday-morning rehearsals are just $10.

CINEMA

Watch flicks downtown at **Teton Theatre** (120 N. Cache Dr.) and **Jackson Hole Twin Cinema** (295 W. Pearl St.), or south of town at **MovieWorks** (860 S. U.S. Hwy. 89). All three of these have the same movie line: 307/733-4939. Find this week's films online at www.jacksonholecinemas.com.

CHUCK-WAGON COOKOUTS

Jackson Hole is home to several chuck-wagon affairs offering all-you-can-eat barbecue cookouts and Western musical performances in the summer. Each has its own advantages, but reservations are highly recommended at all of these.

Run by the Thomas family since 1973, **Bar-T-Five** (790 Cache Creek Rd., 307/733-5386 or 800/772-5386, www.bart5.com, $43 adults, $36 ages 5–12, free for kids under five) is one of the best chuck-wagon feeds. Horse-drawn Conestoga-style wagons depart just east of Snow King, carrying visitors along Cache Creek past costumed mountain men, cowboys, and Indians. At the in-the-trees cookout site (chicken, roast beef, salad, rolls, corn, beans, dessert, and lemonade), cowboys serenade your meal, tell stories, and crack corny jokes that aren't entirely politically correct. It's great fun for families and busloads of Japanese tourists. It's open mid-May–September, with departures Monday–Saturday at 5 and 6:30 P.M. (closed Sun.).

Along the Teton Village Road near Teton Pines, the **Bar J Chuckwagon** (307/733-3370 or 800/905-2275, www.barjchuckwagon.com) does a land-office business throughout the summer, with seating for over 700 people in a cavernous building, including busloads of gray-haired Gray Liners. In existence since 1977, Bar J is famous for its first-rate musicians who fiddle (one is a two-time national fiddle champion), sing, yodel, and regale the audience with cornball jokes and dollops of cowboy poetry. Before the show everyone queues up for heaping servings of barbecued beef, roast chicken, pork rib, or rib-eye steak served with baked potatoes, beans, biscuits, applesauce, spice cake, and lemonade (but no alcohol). Amazingly, Bar

J manages to feed the entire crowd in a half-hour. The picnic-table seating is cramped, but after dinner you're treated to 90 minutes of rollicking entertainment. The cost is $20–30 for adults (depending on your meal), $10 for kids under eight, or free for tots. Bar J is open late May–September, with dinner at 7 P.M.; many folks arrive an hour or so earlier to get front-row seats for the show. It's a good idea to make reservations at least one week ahead. The Bar J does not offer wagon or horseback rides.

In beautiful Buffalo Valley, 45 miles northeast of Jackson, **Castagno Outfitters Covered Wagon Cookouts** (307/543-2407 or 877/559-3585, www.castagnooutfitters.com) start with a 30-minute ride in covered wagons. The wagons stop at an isolated aspen grove, where guests enjoy a dinner of steak, barbecued beans, baked potato, corn bread, watermelon, and dessert. Dinners cost $35 adults, $30 kids, and run mid-June–late August; closed Sunday. Call the day before for reservations.

EVENTS

Jackson Hole is packed with entertaining events almost every day of the year. Some of these are homegrown affairs such as the county fair, whereas others attract people from near and far. Of particular note are the International Pedigree Stage Stop Sled Dog Race (IPSSSDR), the Pole-Pedal-Paddle Race, the Elk Antler Auction, the Grand Teton Music Festival, and the Jackson Hole Fall Arts Festival. (In addition to the events listed, Grand Targhee Ski Resort has a year-round calendar of events on the other side of the Tetons.)

Winter

December is a particularly beautiful time in downtown Jackson. Lights decorate the elk antler arches, and a variety of events take place. Buy arts and crafts during the **Christmas Bazaar** early in the month, or take the kids to visit Saint Nick and his elves on Town Square starting in mid-December; they're there daily 5–7 P.M.

Kick the year off by watching (or participating in) the annual **torchlight ski parades** at all three local ski areas. Parades take place on New Year's Eve at Snow King (400 E. Snow King Ave., 307/733-5200 or 800/522-5464, www.snowking.com) and New Year's Day at Jackson Hole Mountain Resort (307/733-2292 or 888/333-7766, www.jacksonhole.com), where kids have a separate "glow worm" parade using glow sticks. Two parades occur at Grand Targhee Ski Resort (in Alta, 307/353-2300 or 800/827-4433, www.grandtarghee.com) on Christmas Eve and New Year's Eve.

In existence since 1996, the **International Pedigree Stage Stop Sled Dog Race** (IPSSSDR, pronounced IPS-der, 307/734-1163, www.wyomingstagestop.org) is the largest sled dog race in the lower 48 states and a qualifying event for Alaska's Iditarod. Unlike the Iditarod and most other mushing events, this one is run in short 30- to 60-mile legs, with teams operating from a different town each day. As with the Tour de France, it's the total time that counts in this stage race. The race is the creation of Iditarod musher Frank Teasley and nurse Jayne Ottman, who came up with the idea as a way to raise awareness of the need to immunize children; it's unofficially called "The Race to Immunize." IPSSSDR starts in Jackson and then goes on to Lander, Pinedale, Big Piney, Alpine, Kemmerer, and Evanston, before ending in Park City, Utah. The race boasts a $50,000 purse and has attracted some of the top names in dog mushing, including Iditarod winners Lance Mackey, Jeff King, and Rick Swenson. It's held over eight days in late January and early February.

Each February, local Shriners hold horse-drawn **cutter races** (307/733-4052)—essentially a wild chariot race on 0.25 mile of ice—at Melody Ranch, six miles south of Jackson.

Ski and snowboard races take place all winter long at local resorts; volunteer to work one of the gates at a downhill race and you get to ski free the rest of the day.

One of the most popular—and silliest—Jackson events is the **World Championship Snowmobile Hill Climb** (www.snowdevils.org), in which man (or woman) and machine

© KATHY ERICKSON/WILD ABOUT LIFE PHOTOGRAPHY

elk antler auction during Elkfest

churn up the slopes at Snow King Resort. The event takes place in late March.

The ski season ends the first weekend of April with the **Pole-Pedal-Paddle Race** (307/733-6433, www.polepedalpaddle.com), combining alpine skiing, cross-country skiing, cycling, and canoeing in a wild, tough competition. It's the largest such event in the West and great fun for spectators and contestants, many of whom dress up in goofy costumes.

Spring

Spring in Jackson Hole is the least favorite time of the year for many locals. The snow is going, leaving behind brown grass and trees; biking and hiking trails aren't yet passable; and the river is too cold to enjoy. For many folks, this is the time to load up the car and head to Utah for a desert hike in Canyonlands. Despite these conditions, April and May can be a good time to visit, especially if you want to avoid the crowds, need to save money on lodging, or are planning to stay for the summer and need a job and a place to live. (Housing gets progressively more difficult to find after April.)

Summer

Summer begins with a series of events during **Elkfest** (307/733-3316, www.elkfest.org) on the third weekend of May, including a **mountain-man rendezvous** and chili cook-off. The main event, however, is the world's only public **elk antler auction,** which attracts hundreds of buyers from all over the globe to Jackson's Town Square. Local Boy Scouts collect five tons of antlers from the nearby National Elk Refuge each spring, with 80 percent of the proceeds helping to fund feeding of the elk. This may sound like an odd event, but the take is generally more than $60,000! Prices average $9 per pound, and the bidding gets highly competitive; perfectly matched pairs can go for more than $1,500. The antlers are primarily used in taxidermy, belt buckles, and furniture.

Memorial Day weekend in May brings **Old West Days** (307/733-3316), complete with a mountain-man rendezvous, horse-drawn parade, brewfest, carriage show, and crafts fair. In late June, the **Jackson Hole Writers Conference** (307/413-3332, www.

© DON PITCHER

calf roping at Jackson Hole Rodeo

jacksonholewritersconference.com) attracts nationally known authors and wannabes to the Center for the Arts.

Fourth of July is another big event in Jackson, with a parade, rodeo, pancake breakfast, and an impressive fireworks show from Snow King Mountain. Another very popular Independence Day event is the free **Music in the Hole** (307/733-1128, www.gtmf.org) outdoor classical concert by the Grand Teton Music Festival orchestra.

If you have a burning desire for something hot, don't miss the **Jackson Hole Fire Festival** (www.vista360.org) on summer solstice (June 21), when the city partners with Fujiyoshida, Japan. You'll see traditional Japanese drumming, dancing, street torches, and food.

On Wednesday and Saturday nights in summer you can watch bucking broncs, bull riders, barrel racers, rodeo clowns, and hard-riding cowboys at the **Jackson Hole Rodeo** (307/733-7927, www.jacksonholerodeo.us, late May–early Sept., starting at 8 P.M., $14 adults, $9 ages 5–12, free for kids under five) on the Teton County Fair Grounds. Kids get to join

in the amusing calf scramble. Another ongoing event is the **Grand Teton Music Festival** (307/733-1128, www.gtmf.org), providing summertime classical music at Teton Village.

The **Art Fair of Jackson Hole** (307/733-8792, www.jhartfair.org) features more than 100 artisans displaying their works at Miller Park. This highly competitive, juried event takes place in mid-July and again in mid-August.

The last week of July brings an always fun **Teton County Fair** (307/733-5289, www.tetoncountyfair.com) with 4-H exhibits (from lambs to photography), pig wrestling in the mud, a horse show, pony rides and a petting farm, watermelon- and pie-eating contests, live music and comedy acts, a carnival, rodeos, and everyone's favorite: a bang-up **demolition derby** on the final Sunday night.

During the second weekend of September, the invitation-only **Jackson Hole One-Fly Contest** (307/203-2654, www.jhonefly.com) attracts anglers from all over, including several celebrity competitors. Another charity event is **Old Bill's Fun Run** (307/739-1026, www.oldbills.org) the second Saturday of September; it's raised more than $67 million over the last decade or so!

Fall

Jackson Hole is at its most glorious in the fall, as aspens and cottonwoods turn into a fire of yellow and orange against the Teton backdrop. Most tourists have fled back home, leaving locals and hardier visitors to savor the cool autumn nights. The peak time for **fall colors** is generally the first week of October—considerably later than most people expect.

The primary autumn event is the **Jackson Hole Fall Arts Festival** (307/733-3316, www.jacksonholechamber.com/events), which takes place over a 10-day period in September. Featured activities include exhibits at the National Museum of Wildlife Art and local galleries, a juried art fair, an art auction, Western fashion and furniture shows, a miniature art show, cowboy poetry and old-time cowboy music, "Taste of the Tetons" with delectable food from local restaurants, and tours of historic ranches. Also fun is a "quickdraw" in which artists paint, draw, and sculpt while you watch; the pieces are then auctioned off.

In early October, **Quilting in the Tetons** (307/733-3087, www.quiltthetetons.org) brings a week of exhibits, classes, workshops, and quilting demonstrations.

Shopping

If you have the money (or a credit card), Jackson is a great place to buy everything from artwork to mountain bikes. Even if you just hitchhiked in and have no cash to spare, it's always fun to wander through the shops and galleries surrounding Town Square.

Fans of classic Old West furniture should not miss **Fighting Bear Antiques** (375 S. Cache, 307/733-2669 or 866/690-2669, www.fightingbear.com), famed for its collection of Thomas Molesworth pieces. It's housed in a huge log structure a few blocks from Town Square. Owner Terry Winchell literally wrote the book on this creator of uniquely American furniture.

There are lots of T-shirt places in town, but **Lee's Tees** (80 W. Broadway Ave/, 307/733-6671, www.leestees.com) sells the high-quality versions.

OUTDOOR GEAR

Outdoor enthusiasts will discover several excellent shops in Jackson. Climbers, backpackers, and cross-country skiers head to America's oldest climbing shop, **Teton Mountaineering** (170 N. Cache Dr., 307/733-3595 or 800/850-3595, www.tetonmtn.com), for quality equipment, maps, and travel guides. They also rent tents, sleeping bags, pads, backpacks, climbing shoes, crampons, and ice axes in the summer, along with snowshoes and cross-country, telemark, and alpine touring skis in winter. Check the bulletin board for used items.

Jack Dennis Sports (50 E. Broadway Ave., 307/733-3270 or 800/570-3270, www.jackdennisoutdoors.com) is a large upscale store with fly-fishing and camping gear in summer and skis and warm clothes during winter. The store also rents almost anything: tents, stoves, lanterns, cookware, sleeping bags, fishing poles, fly rods, waders, float tubes, backpacks, skis, snowboards, snowshoes, and more.

Skinny Skis (65 W. Deloney Ave., 307/733-6094 or 888/733-7205, www.skinnyskis.com) has high-quality clothing and supplies, especially cross-country ski gear. Rent sleeping bags, tents, climbing shoes, ice axes, baby carriers, and backpacks here. The same folks run the summer-only **Moosely Seconds** (307/739-1801) in Moose, with climbing and outdoor gear, along with rentals of trekking poles, ice axes, crampons, rock shoes, approach shoes, plastic boots, and snowshoes.

Another place to rent outdoor gear of all

types—including fishing gear, tents, sleeping bags, kayaks, float tubes, dry suits, water skis, backpacks, camp stoves, and lanterns—is **Leisure Sports** (1075 S. U.S. Hwy. 89, 307/733-3040, www.leisuresportsadventure.com).

Teton Adventure Gear (220 E. Broadway Ave., 307/203-2915, www.tetonadventuregear.com) rents spotting scopes, binoculars, GPS units, bear spray, electric bear fences, tents, bike racks, avalanche air bags(!), and unique rooftop car tents.

Gart Sports (485 W. Broadway Ave., 307/733-4449, www.gartsports.com) is a large store with a variety of outdoor and sports gear.

The least expensive place to buy rugged outdoor wear, cowboy boots, and cowboy hats is **Boot Barn** (840 W. Broadway Ave., 307/733-0247, www.bootbarn.com).

BARGAINS

Buy used clothing and other items at **Browse 'N Buy Thrift Shop** (139 N. Cache Dr., 307/733-7524) or the more chaotic **Orville's** (385 N. Cache Dr., 307/733-2684).

BOOKS

Unlike many Wyoming towns where the book selection consists of a few bodice-buster romance novels in the local pharmacy, Jackson is blessed with several fine bookstores. **Valley Bookstore** (125 N. Cache Dr., 307/733-4533, www.valleybookstore.com) is the largest local bookshop, with a big choice of regional titles, plus occasional author signings and readings. **Main Event** (980 W. Broadway Ave., 307/733-7112) in the Powderhorn Mall sells new books and CDs and rents videos. A few doors away in the mall is **Jackson Hole Book Traders** (307/734-6001, www.jacksonholebooktraders.com), with a surprising selection of used and rare books. Find a great selection of regional and natural history titles at **Jackson Hole and Greater Yellowstone Visitor Center** (532 N. Cache Dr., 307/733-3316, www.jacksonholechamber.com).

Accommodations

As one of the premier centers for tourism in Wyoming, Jackson Hole is jam-packed with more than 70 different motels, hotels, and B&Bs, plus many more condominiums and guest ranches. Other lodging can be found just to the north within or near Grand Teton National Park. The Jackson Hole Chamber of Commerce's website (www.jacksonholechamber.com) has brief descriptions and Web links for most local places.

Because of the town's popularity, Jackson accommodations command premium prices. With a few exceptions, you'll pay at least $110 d during the peak visitor seasons of July–August and late December–early January. Rates can drop more than 50 percent in the off-season, so if you can visit March–May or late September–mid-December, you'll save a lot of cash. (The same Super 8 Motel rooms that go for $179 in July cost just $63 in early November!) In the town of Jackson, the highest rates are usually in July and August, while at Teton Village, skiers and snowboarders send room rates to their peak between mid-December and early January. You will need to add 6 percent in taxes to all the lodging rates below, and some hotels also add a 2 percent "resort impact fee" for regional marketing.

Reservations are highly recommended. For midsummer, book rooms at least two months ahead, or longer if you really want to be certain of a place. During the Christmas–New Year's period you should probably reserve six months in advance to ensure a spot. Summer weekends tend to be the most crowded, with many families driving up from Salt Lake City for a cooling break in the mountains.

If you're overwhelmed by all the lodging choices, try one of the reservation services, such as **Jackson Hole Central Reservations**

(307/733-4005 or 800/443-6931, www.jacksonholewy.com). Looking for other opinions? Tripadvisor (www.tripadvisor.com) has many reviews of Jackson Hole lodging places.

JACKSON HOTELS AND MOTELS
Under $100

Two older motels—The Cottages at Snow King and Alpine Motel—offer the cheapest rates in town and have the same owners. Both are located in quiet residential areas, but they don't take advance reservations and are often booked up by summertime workers. They're a good last-minute option if you roll into town without reservations and not a lot of cash. The modest rooms at **The Cottages at Snow King** (470 King St., 307/733-3480, $88–98 d) include one or two queen beds, a fridge, and microwave; full kitchen units ($120) sleep four. Pets are welcome at no extra charge. **Alpine Motel** (70 S. Jean St., 307/739-3200, $82–92 d, $110 for kitchen units) is just a few blocks from Town Square. The furnishings may not be the newest, but the rooms are clean, and a small outdoor pool (heated seasonally) is on the premises. Both motels rent rooms only on a monthly basis October–April.

Family-owned **(Kudar Motel** (260 N. Cache Dr., 307/733-2823, www.kudarmotel.com, $89 d, early May–early Oct.) is a holdover from a quieter era when Jackson's motels were simple and unpretentious. You'll find 14 basic motel units with queen- or king-size beds and TVs; three rooms contain the original 1950s furnishings. Of considerably more interest are Kudar's 17 rustic but nicely maintained and spotless log cabins ($109–129 d), built in 1938. The larger two-room cabins can sleep five. There are no phones in any of the units, but the cabins contain fridges, microwaves, air conditioning, and Wi-Fi. There's a large grassy center with shady trees. Travelers love Kudar's, with many returning year after year, including some who've visited annually since the 1950s.

$100-200

Many Jackson accommodations fall in the $100–200 range, with pricing factors being location, type of room, quality of furnishings, and presence of amenities such as pools and hot tubs. Most are comfortable midrange options, not corporate lodging giants, but they offer good value and down-home friendliness.

DOWNTOWN

Justifiably popular with families, **Elk Country Inn** (480 W. Pearl, 307/733-2364 or 800/483-8667, www.elkcountryinn.com) is a fine option. Choose from spacious motel rooms ($140 s or $146 d) with two queen beds, fridge, and microwave, or a room with three queen beds, one of which is in an upstairs loft ($166 d or $185 for six guests). (Add $10 to these prices for a kitchenette unit.) There's also a luxury suite ($210 d) with a king bed and kitchen. Out back are two dozen modern log cabins ($194–214 d) with full kitchenettes, including dishes and lodgepole furnishings. Guests appreciate the indoor hot tub, exercise room, shady picnic area with a small playground, Wi-Fi, plus a free wintertime shuttle to Teton Village. Elk Country is one of the better bargains in Jackson.

Located in a peaceful neighborhood six blocks from Town Square, family-owned **(Buckrail Lodge** (110 E. Karns Ave., 307/733-2079, www.buckraillodge.com, $111 d with one queen, $137 d with two queen beds) has faux-log-cabin units on immaculate parklike grounds; portions of Clint Eastwood's *Any Which Way You Can* were filmed here. Relax in the large outdoor hot tub, then plunk down for the night in one of the dozen lovingly maintained motel rooms, all decorated with Western-style furnishings. There are no in-room phones (use your cell phone) and the walls are thin, but the bathrooms are spacious and guests can use the computer in the lobby or open a laptop for Wi-Fi. Buckrail is closed mid-October–April.

At **Anvil Motel** (215 N. Cache Dr., 307/733-3668 or 800/234-4507, www.anvilmotel.com), stay in a little room with one queen ($128 d) or relax in a larger unit with two queen beds ($148 for up to four people). A Jacuzzi suite ($192) and family suite ($310) are also available. All rooms include a microwave, small fridge, and Wi-Fi. The same owners run the nearby **El Rancho Motel** (240 N. Glenwood Dr., 307/733-3668 or 800/234-4507, www.anvilmotel.com, $104–137 d) with older budget units and no air-conditioning.

Ranch Inn (45 E. Pearl St., 307/733-6363 or 800/348-5599, www.ranchinn.com) offers a wide variety of accommodations just one block off Town Square. These include standard rooms ($115 d), tower rooms with balconies facing Snow King, fridges, and microwaves ($160 d), and suites with king beds, wood-burning fireplaces, balconies, and jetted tubs ($180 d). Amenities include an indoor hot tub, Wi-Fi, and a continental breakfast. Some tower rooms are wheelchair-accessible.

Golden Eagle Inn (325 E. Broadway Ave., 307/733-2042 or 888/748-6937, www.goldeneagleinn.com) is a quiet, out-of-the-way family motel with standard rooms for $140 d, and larger rooms for $160–190 d. All include a microwave, small refrigerator, Wi-Fi, and access to a heated outdoor pool. Adjacent is a two-bedroom house with a full kitchen that sleeps four for $275. The same owner has **Four Winds Motel** (150 N. Millward St., 307/733-2474 or 800/228-6461, www.jacksonholefourwinds.com, $125 d), just a few blocks from Town Square and across the street from a city park (with a popular children's playground). The rooms are nothing fancy, but they're exceptionally clean and affordably priced. Free Wi-Fi. Both Golden Eagle and Four Winds are open April–November.

A couple of blocks off Town Square, cozy **Anglers Inn** (265 N. Millward St., 307/733-3682 or 800/867-4667, www.anglersinn.net, $140–160 d) has pleasant rooms with Western-style fixtures, lodgepole beds and chairs, and small baths. All rooms contain a fridge, microwave, and free Wi-Fi.

Find a diverse mixture of room styles at

Jackson Hole Lodge (420 W. Broadway Ave., 307/733-2992 or 800/604-9404, www. jacksonholelodge.com), where featured attractions are a large indoor swimming pool, a wading pool, two hot tubs, a sauna, Wi-Fi, a guest computer, and a game room on attractive grounds. Standard motel rooms cost $109–139 d. Condo-type units are much nicer, with an upscale decor that includes log furniture; they're $169 for a studio unit, $269 for a one-bedroom unit (sleeps four to six) with a living room, fireplace, and full kitchen. Two-bedroom units cost $329 for up to eight people.

Antler Inn (50 W. Pearl Ave., 307/733-2535 or 800/522-2406, www.townsquareinns.com) is a large 110-room property just one block off Town Square. Many units contain two queen beds ($150 d), but also available are a dozen large family rooms/suites ($190–275) with three beds and space for six people. Most of these have wood-burning fireplaces. Rounding out the options are attractive (but small) log-walled rooms ($130 d). All guests have access to an exercise room, sauna, large indoor hot tub, and Wi-Fi. There's a free winter shuttle to Teton Village.

Rawhide Motel (75 S. Millward St., 307/733-1216, www.rawhidemotel.com, $159 d) is a fine midtown place with large rooms containing handmade lodgepole furniture, plus Wi-Fi and fridges. Open early May–early October.

The rooms are a bit cramped, but guests appreciate the friendly service and extra touches at **Sundance Inn** (135 W. Broadway Ave., 307/733-3444, www.sundanceinnjackson. com). The motel is close to Town Square and serves a light homemade breakfast plus evening cookies and lemonade. Standard rooms cost $139–159 d ($129 for two twin beds), while two-room suites are $185 for up to four people. Wi-Fi is available.

On the north side of town, **Cache Creek Lodge** (390 N. Glenwood, 307/733-7781, www.cachecreekmotel.com) is another well-kept, moderately priced choice. All rooms include full kitchens (with dishes and pans) and Wi-Fi. Standard units start at $140 d, with two-bedroom suites that sleep up to six for $185 d.

A large heart-of-town place is **49'er Inn and Suites/Quality Inn** (330 W. Pearl, 307/733-7550 or 800/451-2980, www.49erinn.com), with 142 rooms spread across several buildings. There are standard rooms ($165 d) with two queen beds and a nothing-special decor; newer and considerably nicer are five-person studio suites ($220, some include fireplaces); and two luxury suites ($245) with hot tub and fireplace. Final options include a three-bedroom apartment and two-bedroom house (both $339). All guests have access to outdoor and indoor hot tubs, sauna, and exercise room, plus a full breakfast and Wi-Fi.

SOUTHSIDE

On the south end of Jackson at the Y intersection of highways 89 and 22, **Pony Express Motel** (1075 W. Broadway Ave., 307/733-3835 or 800/526-2658, www.ponyexpressmotel.com) is an excellent family option. Kitchen units with a queen bed are $139 d, while family units with a queen bed and a bunk bed for the kids, plus microwave and fridge, cost $149. Free Wi-Fi, but the main attraction is a heated outdoor pool.

Right across the highway from Pony Express, **Teton Gables Motel** (1140 W. Broadway Ave., 307/733-3723, www.tetongables.com, $124 d) is another reasonably priced place with older rooms, all with microwave, fridge, and free Wi-Fi.

One of Jackson's better deals for standard motel rooms is—not surprisingly—**Motel 6** (1370 W. Broadway Ave., 307/733-1620 or 800/466-8356, www.motel6.com, $106 d), but even here the summertime rates are high. You'll find humdrum rooms and an outdoor pool; reserve six months in advance for July and August. Off-season prices ($40 d) are a much better bargain.

NORTHSIDE

Two mid-priced motels are adjacent to each other, one mile north of Jackson on U.S. 89. Both face the Elk Refuge (and the busy highway). **Elk Refuge Inn** (307/733-3582 or 800/544-3582, www.elkrefugeinn.com) is the smaller and more homey of the two, with a mix of rooms and friendly management. Rates are $135 d for downstairs rooms or $150 for upstairs units with kitchenettes and private balconies. A six-person family unit is $140. All rooms include drive-up access, fridge, microwave, continental breakfast, Wi-Fi, and guest computer.

Flat Creek Inn (307/733-5276 or 800/438-9338, www.flatcreekinn.com) is a large two-level motel just a few hundred feet north of Elk Refuge Inn. Rooms are functionally furnished, with microwaves and small fridges. Standard rooms are $169 for up to four guests, while spacious kitchenettes sleep up to five for $209. Three suites ($149–319) are more spacious, and the largest includes a separate bedroom with king bed, kitchen, flat-screen TV, and other comforts. Guests in the suites have access to an indoor hot tub, and all guests get a continental breakfast and Wi-Fi in the lobby.

Over $200

It should come as no surprise that tony Jackson Hole has several elaborate, pricey, and sumptuous places to stay, with rooms starting around $200 and hitting the stratosphere at $4,000 a night!

DOWNTOWN

Close to Town Square, the **Wort Hotel** (50 N. Glenwood St., 307/733-2190 or 800/322-2727, www.worthotel.com) has been a Jackson favorite since 1941. A disastrous 1980 fire—started by a bird that built a nest too close to a neon sign—destroyed the roof and upper floor. The hotel was completely restored within a year, and today it's better than ever, with such amenities as a fitness center, valet parking, Wi-Fi, a business center, and two small hot tubs. The lobby, with its grand central staircase and stone fireplace with crackling fire, makes a fine place to meet friends. The Silver Dollar Bar and Grill serves meals, or you can sidle up to the famous curving bar—inlaid with 2,032 uncirculated silver dollars from 1921. The Wort's spacious rooms are attractively decorated with a New West motif that includes lodgepole-pine beds and creative fixtures. Rates are $349 d for standard rooms (with two queens or one king bed), or $389 d for larger and more luxurious rooms. Spacious junior suites with king beds and wet bars cost $449, while the luxury suite will set you back $799 d.

Greatly expanded and updated in the last few years, **The Lexington at Jackson Hole** (235 N. Cache Dr., 307/733-2648 or 888/771-2648, www.lexjh.com) sprawls across four buildings with very comfortable guest rooms and a friendly staff. Large units with two queen beds or one king bed are $219 d, while two-room suites cost $269 d, or $289 d for units with kitchenettes; add $12 for each additional adult. Amenities include a small indoor family pool and hot tub, a filling hot breakfast, fridges, a computer in the lobby, and Wi-Fi.

An outstanding in-town choice is **Parkway Inn** (125 N. Jackson St., 307/733-3143 or 800/247-8390, www.parkwayinn.com). This immaculate, midsize lodge has a delightful Victorian ambience with antique furniture and quilts in many rooms, along with jetted tubs and flat-screen TVs in the some units. Guests will also enjoy a small indoor lap pool, two hot tubs, two saunas, and a gym in the basement, along with Wi-Fi. A light breakfast is served in the lobby. Rates are $249 d for standard rooms with two queen beds or a king bed, $329 for larger suites, or $369 d for two-room suites; $25 each for additional guests (maximum of four per room).

An excellent nine-room lodge just a few blocks from Town Square, **Inn on the Creek** (295 N. Millward, 307/739-1565 or 800/669-9534, www.innonthecreek.com) has a peaceful location beside Flat Creek. Standard rooms ($229–279 d) feature designer furnishings and down comforters. The deluxe rooms ($299–349 d) also include fireplaces and in-room hot tubs, while a gorgeous suite ($599) sleeps four and has a full kitchen, jetted tub, and private patio. A light breakfast is delivered to your door each morning, and there's a private backyard, Wi-Fi, and guest computer.

Another downtown option is **Grand Victorian Lodge** (85 N. Perry Ave., 307/739-2294 or 800/584-0532, www.grandvictorianlodge.com), a "boutique hotel with a bed and breakfast ambience." Choose from standard rooms ($199–219 d), deluxe rooms ($229–279 d), or a large two-room suite ($289 d) that features a four-poster king bed, jetted tub, and gas fireplace. A delicious full breakfast is a morning highlight, and guests can relax on the back deck or surf the Web wirelessly.

You'll find outdoorsy owners at **Alpine House Country Inn** (285 N. Glenwood, 307/739-1570 or 800/753-1421, www.alpinehouse.com); both Hans and Nancy Johnstone were skiers for U.S. Olympic teams and are highly knowledgeable about adventure options in the Tetons. The timber-frame lodge is just two blocks from Jackson's Town Square and has 22 guest rooms in two connected buildings. Both are bright and modern, accented by Swedish-style stenciling on the walls. All rooms have private balconies and deep soaking tubs, saunas, plus access to a central computer and Wi-Fi. A healthy full buffet breakfast is served. Rates are $175 d in the original rooms (no TV or air conditioning), or $215–260 d in the new building, which also features gas fireplaces in most rooms. The two suites cost $295 for up to four guests. The owners also manage four two-bedroom cottages ($400) nearby that sleep five comfortably; each cottage has two bedrooms, a sleeper sofa, washer, dryer, and kitchen. Closed in November and April.

Acclaimed **◖ Rusty Parrot Lodge and Spa** (175 N. Jackson, 307/733-2000 or 888/739-1749, www.rustyparrot.com) features sumptuous accommodations just two blocks from Town Square. All 31 rooms are highlighted with handcrafted furniture, original artwork, oversize tubs, and goose-down comforters; some also contain wood-burning fireplaces or jetted tubs. Rates are $400–475 d for standard rooms, or $635 d for the luxurious master suite, and include an unforgettable breakfast (it's never the same) served each morning in the cozy dining room. (Deduct $40 from the rate if you don't want the breakfast.) Guests can relax in the hot tub on a deck overlooking Jackson, borrow a book from the library, or pamper themselves with a massage, aromatherapy session, or facial from Body Sage Spa (extra charges). The lodge also serves epicurean dinners at Wild Sage Restaurant (daily 5:30–9:30 P.M.). It doesn't get much better than this.

One of Jackson's newest lodging places is **Homewood Suites by Hilton** (207 N. Millward St., 307/739-0808 or 800/225-5466, www.jacksonwy.homewoodsuites.com, $359–389 d). All units are two-room suites with separate living and sleeping areas, top-of-the-line beds, a fireplace, two TVs and phones, free airport shuttle, an indoor pool, fitness center, and hot tub, plus fully equipped kitchens, Wi-Fi, and a big breakfast buffet. Guests are served a light dinner Monday–Thursday evenings.

SOUTHSIDE

The Point Inn & Suites (1280 W. Broadway Ave., 307/733-0033 or 877/547-5223, www.thepointjh.com) has comfortable rooms at the south end of town. Standard rooms cost $189 d, while Western-style suites with fireplaces and hot tubs go for $239 d. Amenities include a light breakfast, large hot tub, fitness facility, sauna, Wi-Fi, guest computers, ski racks, plus microwaves and fridges in most rooms. (The hotel was formerly a Days Inn.)

A modern hotel with an ostentatious lobby and southside location, **Wyoming Inn of Jackson Hole** (930 W. Broadway Ave., 307/734-0035 or 800/844-0035, www.wyoming-inn.com) has large and comfortable rooms for $299 d, including a big hot breakfast. The finest rooms ($349 d) also include fireplaces and jetted tubs. Guests appreciate Wi-Fi, guest computers, laundry service (a big hit with families), and a free airport shuttle, all at no extra charge.

A three-story building sandwiched between strip malls on the south end of Jackson, **The Lodge at Jackson Hole (Best Western)** (80 S. Scott La., 307/739-9703 or 800/458-3866,

www.lodgeatjh.com) has big guest rooms featuring a fridge, microwave, safe, Wi-Fi, and two queen beds (or a king) for $259 d. Hotel guests are treated to a buffet breakfast, a unique indoor/outdoor heated pool, hot tubs, and a sauna, plus access to the Jackson Hole Athletic Club and a free winter shuttle to Teton Village.

Log Cabin Motels

Several local motels offer log-cabin accommodations for a step back into the Old West while keeping such newer amenities as TVs, private baths, and Wi-Fi.

Set amid tall cottonwood trees along Flat Creek, **Rustic Inn** (475 N. Cache Dr., 307/733-2357 or 800/323-9279, www.rusticinnatjh.com) has a sprawling mixture of cozy log cabins, log-motel units, and newer log-sided units. The website details all cabin choices, ranging from older cabins (containing two queen beds and a fireplace for $229 d) to larger ones (with flat-screen TVs, fridges, and microwaves for $329 d), up to "superior" cabins with private decks, rain showers, flat-screen TVs, and king beds ($399 d). Add $10 per person for additional guests (max. four persons). All guests have access to the sauna, gym, outdoor pool, and hot tub, plus Wi-Fi, concierge service, and a hot breakfast. Guests sometimes complain of the lack of electrical outlets and limited storage for skis and other winter gear.

Near a busy Jackson intersection, **Cowboy Village Resort** (120 Flat Creek Dr., 307/733-3121 or 800/962-4988, www.townsquareinns.com) has 82 modern but jammed-together cabins with kitchenettes and sleeper sofas. The cabins cost $178–198 for up to four people in a studio unit with two queen bunk beds, or $218 for a cabin with a separate bedroom (one king or two queens). Two hotel rooms are available: one with a king bed ($208 d) and a larger unit with two queens, a bunk bed, and full kitchen ($278 for up to six). Guests have access to a covered outdoor pool, an indoor hot tub, office computer, and Wi-Fi. In winter a continental breakfast is available, along with a free shuttle to Teton Village.

TETON VILLAGE HOTELS AND MOTELS

Teton Village is 12 miles northwest of Jackson at the base of Jackson Hole Resort. The Village has a variety of lodging and dining options and year-round activities, and is perfect for skiers and snowboarders. Frequent START bus service makes it easy to get to town, even if you don't have a rental car. Most lodging and dining places are considerably more expensive than in Jackson, but the Village has a couple of lower-priced choices. In addition to hotels in this area, be sure to check out condominium rentals as a Teton Village option.

Under $100

Located in the heart of Teton Village, **The Hostel** (307/733-3415, www.thehostel.us) provides budget rates in a scenic location. Eight coed or single-sex hostel rooms are available for $32 per person; private rooms run $79 s or d, or $89 for up to four people. The tiny plain-vanilla rooms lack TV or phones, but there's a big central lounge for camaraderie; it includes TVs, DVD players, pay phones, pool table, table tennis, foosball, fireplace, microwave, refrigerator, games, Wi-Fi ($5 per day), and a ski-waxing room. Because of its Teton Village location at the foot of Jackson Hole Mountain Resort, The Hostel is very popular with skiers on a budget, so reserve two months ahead for midwinter rooms. Winter reservations require a four-night minimum stay. Space is typically available in the summer, with no minimum stay. Pets are accepted for a $10 fee.

$100-200

In the heart of Teton Village action, **Village Center Inn** (307/733-3990 or 800/443-8613, www.jhrl.com) charges $105 d for studio or loft units and $150 for two-bedroom units that sleep six. All units include full kitchens, but no Wi-Fi (though it's available nearby). Peak-season winter rates rise to $200 d for a one-bedroom unit, and up to $230 for two bedrooms. The decor is utilitarian, but other than The Hostel, this is the cheapest Teton Village accommodation. There is a two-night minimum stay in winter.

$200-300

Alpenhof Lodge (307/733-3242 or 800/732-3244, www.alpenhoflodge.com) exudes a European ambience, reflecting its Swiss and German owners. Summertime rates start at $239 d for the simplest rooms on the top floor with sloping ceilings, or $289 for rooms with Bavarian furnishings and space for four guests. A two-room suite is $549. A continental breakfast is included and guests have access to the heated year-round outdoor pool, hot tub, sauna, Wi-Fi, and computer. The resident golden retrievers are a bonus.

Another Teton Village option, **The Inn at Jackson Hole/Best Western** (307/733-2311 or 800/842-7666, www.innatjh.com) has standard rooms with log furnishings ($209–219 d), units with kitchenettes and fireplaces ($239–269 d), and family-friendly loft suites with fireplaces and kitchenettes ($329 for up to four guests). Guests can use the hotel's outdoor heated pool and hot tub, sauna, and ski lockers. There's an upscale restaurant and Wi-Fi.

Over $300

If you're looking for beautifully appointed accommodations, you can't go wrong at **C** **Snake River Lodge and Spa** (307/732-6000 or 800/445-4655, www.snakeriver-lodge.rockresorts.com). The lodge features a New West–style lobby with stone fireplaces and whimsically carved bears, plus rooms that follow the theme with rustic lamps, pine furniture, and colorful prints. A distinctive free-form indoor/outdoor heated pool has a cascading waterfall, and other attractions include indoor and outdoor hot tubs, a sauna, ski lockers, a ski-in concierge service, Wi-Fi, and a five-story spa and health club with exercise equipment, facials, manicures, hydrotherapy, massages, soaking tubs, and steam baths. Peak-season summer and winter rates are around $345 d for the guest rooms, $665 d for a one-bedroom suite or condo, up to $1,575 for a three-bedroom private home. Snake River

Lodge is owned by RockResorts; their website frequently offers multi-night specials that include breakfast.

Four Seasons Resort (307/732-5000, www.fourseasons.com/jacksonhole) includes a 124-room luxury hotel with ski-in access, an elegant restaurant (Westbank Grill), an après-ski bar for slope-side drinks, a gorgeous outdoor heated pool, three hot tubs, a full health club, spa, and concierge all under one roof. Summertime rates start at $695 d for not-so-standard standard rooms (king bed, marble bath and soaking tub, in-room safe, minibar, private terrace or gas fireplace). Also available are 32 condos and homes, including a five-bedroom place that rents for $7,500 a night in the ski season!

Another of Jackson Hole's upmarket lodging options (it gets a four-diamond rating from AAA), **Teton Mountain Lodge** (307/734-7111 or 800/801-6615, www.tetonmountainlodge. com) is a Western-style lodge at the base of the mountain in Teton Village. An impressive array of amenities and services are featured: indoor and outdoor heated pools, hot tubs (including an amazing adults-only rooftop version), a fitness center/spa, concierge service, valet parking, Wi-Fi, and underground parking. Guests can choose from lodge rooms or studios ($309–319 d), junior suites ($389 d), one-, two-, or three-bedroom suites ($529–1,330 d), all the way up to the penthouse suite ($1,830 nightly).

One of the newer high-end lodges in Teton Village, **Hotel Terra** (307/739-4000 or 800/631-6281, www.hotelterrajacksonhole. com) has a splashy modern design with an eco-boutique emphasis. Rooms are sumptuously appointed, with organic cotton sheets and bathrobes, Wi-Fi, safes, twice-daily maid service, and all sorts of techie treats, from "rain showers" in the bath and in-floor heating to iPod docking stations and flat-screen TVs. Guests have access to the pools, fitness center, and hot tubs at adjacent Teton Mountain Lodge (same owners). Standard rooms are $319–329 d, studios with kitchens cost $339

d, and suites start at $530–975 d, up to a magnificent three-bedroom suite for $1,545.

BED-AND-BREAKFASTS

Jackson hosts many fine B&Bs, where those who can afford it can relax in comfort at the homes of locals. Be sure to reserve space far ahead during the peak summer season, although you might get lucky at the last minute if someone cancels. The **Jackson Hole Bed and Breakfast Association's** website (www. jacksonholebnb.com) has links to a number of local B&Bs.

Teton Village

Near the Aspens along the road to Teton Village, **The Sassy Moose Inn** (307/733-1277, www.sassymoose.com, $159–189 d) is a modest log house with five guest rooms, each with private bath, TV, and Wi-Fi. The larger rooms have two beds and are fine for families. A full breakfast is served each morning. Guests can soak in the outdoor hot tub, and an on-site spa provides massage and other treats. Pets are welcome (a rarity for B&Bs).

On the way to Teton Village, **Teton View B&B** (2136 Coyote Loop, 307/733-7954, www. tetonview.com) features a guest room ($225 d) and suite ($259 d), both with private baths. Guests enjoy a big breakfast, Wi-Fi, and a dramatic view of the Tetons from both the indoor whirlpool tub and outdoor hot tub. The owners also offer a perfect-for-families cabin with a kitchen, wood-burning stove, and private bath ($325 d). For additional guests, add $25 per adult or $15 per child. A two-night minimum stay is required. Open June–October.

The rambling **Wildflower Inn** (307/733-4710 or 888/893-7910, www.jacksonholewildflower.com) sits on three acres of country land along Teton Village Road, with five bright guest rooms. Four rooms have private decks, and all contain private baths and handcrafted lodgepole beds. One of the rooms is actually a suite with a separate sitting room, hot tub, and gas fireplace. Ken and Sherrie Jern built and manage the B&B, and bring a wealth of local knowledge; both were ski instructors at Vail, and he's a longtime Exum climbing guide. Rates are $300–350 d ($380 d for the suite) and include a memorable family-style breakfast and a plant-filled solarium. Children are welcome, and Wi-Fi is available.

One of the most impressive local lodging options is ⟨ **Bentwood B&B** (307/739-1411, www.bentwoodinn.com), just north of the junction on the road to Teton Village. This massive 6,000-square-foot log home sits amid tall cottonwood trees and is a favorite place for weddings and receptions. The interior is filled with Western styling and English antiques. The grand living room is centered on a three-story stone fireplace, and each of the five elegant guest rooms has a fireplace, flat-screen TV, deck or balcony, jetted tub, and Wi-Fi. The loft room is perfect for families. Innkeepers Deborah and Lee Clukey are gracious hosts. Wine and hors d'oeuvres are served each evening, and morning brings a creative breakfast. Lodging rates are $350 d, or $450 for up to four in the family room. Children are welcome in this very special place.

Wilson

A personal favorite is **Teton Treehouse B&B** (307/733-3233, www.atetontreehouse-jackson-hole.com, $215–240 d) a gorgeous four-story hillside home in Wilson. This spacious open-beam B&B sits up 95 steps—needless to say, it's not accessible for people with disabilities—and contains six guest rooms with private baths. It really does offer the feeling of living in a tree house, and it's a great place for bird-watchers. Decks provide impressive views across the valley below, and guests enjoy a healthy full breakfast each morning along with Wi-Fi access and a popular evening fire pit. Young children are not permitted, and there's a three-night minimum stay in July and August. The B&B is open mid-May–September.

RESORTS
Jackson

At the base of Jackson's in-town ski hill, and just a few blocks from downtown, **Snow King Resort** (400 E. Snow King Ave., 307/733-5200 or 800/522-5464, www.snowking.com) includes more than 200 hotel rooms and 170 condos, plus such amenities as a year-round heated outdoor pool, hot tub, sauna, exercise facility, restaurants facing the slopes, a bar, concierge, business center, game room, spa, and Wi-Fi. A free shuttle provides connections to the airport and Teton Village (winters), and guests receive discounted passes for Snow King Ski Area. The lodge offers reasonable ski-and-stay packages starting at $140 per night for two people, including lodging, breakfast, and a ski pass in early winter. When the snow is gone, Snow King is a popular destination for meetings, offering 48,000 square feet of conference space. A winter ice rink is close by, and in summer a slide, horseback riding, chairlift, bike trails, and miniature golf course attract families. The main resort building has a 1970s feel, but guest rooms are comfortable and updated. Hotel rooms at Snow King cost $245 d in the summer, with condos starting around $300 d, up to an ultra-luxurious three-bedroom Love Ridge condo that will set you back $745 per night.

Some of the most dramatic vistas of the Tetons are from the luxurious **Spring Creek Ranch** (307/733-8833 or 800/443-6139, www.springcreekranch.com). On a 1,000-acre estate, the resort sits high atop Gros Ventre Butte four miles west of Jackson and includes a wide range of lodging options. Hotel rooms and studios are $340 d in the summer, and two-bedroom suites cost $360 for four people. One-bedroom condos run $340 d; two- and three-bedroom condos range from $410 to $1,400 nightly, with the largest sleeping eight comfortably. Also available are executive four-bedroom homes (one covers 6,500 square feet!) that cost a mere $2,250 per night. All rooms at Spring Creek Ranch contain fireplaces and lodgepole furnishings, and the condos and studios include full kitchens. Other amenities include a private pond, tennis courts, an outdoor pool, hot tub, fitness center, courtesy airport

© DON PITCHER

Spring Creek Ranch

transportation, and day spa with massage and other offerings (extra fee).

Atop Gros Ventre Butte near Spring Creek Ranch is stunning **Amangani** (307/734-7333 or 877/734-7333, www.amangani.com), the only representative of Amanresorts in America. (Most of the company's other lavish resorts are in Asia.) Aman groupies and business travelers know to expect the utmost in luxury, and they will certainly not be disappointed here, starting with dressed-in-black employees and spare-no-expenses construction. Guests who come here expect pampering, and the somewhat snooty staff obliges. The three-story sandstone-faced hotel contains 40 suites, each with a patinaed-metal fireplace, mountain-facing balcony, king-size bed, deep soaking tub (with a window view), minibar, and terrazzo dining table. Amangani's central lobby is particularly impressive, blending sandstone columns, redwood accents, custom furnishings, and soaring two-story windows. Outside, those soaking in a whirlpool and heated 35-meter pool enjoy a remarkable view of the Tetons. Among other amenities are a complete health center, a gourmet restaurant, a lounge, and courtesy airport transportation. Amangani's accommodations include suites ($875 d), three deluxe suites ($1,100 d), five large luxury suites with two baths and spacious balconies ($1,400–1,700 d), and a four-bedroom home ($4,800) for the utmost in sumptuousness. A three-night minimum is required in the summer. The health center and restaurant are open to the general public.

Teton Village

Four miles south of Teton Village, **Teton Pines Resort and Country Club** (307/733-1005 or 800/238-2223, www.tetonpines.com) features the amenities you'd expect in a year-round resort, including an 18-hole golf course, tennis center, and classy restaurant. Guests have access to the outdoor pool and hot tub, athletic-club privileges, concierge service, and an airport shuttle. Most of the resort's condos are privately owned, but three large (2,100-square-foot) three-bedroom town houses are offered on a nightly basis. Each includes a kitchen, dining room, two decks, three baths, a fireplace, hot tub, washer, dryer, and attached garage. These sleep up to eight for $1,050 per night. Golf packages are also available.

GUEST RANCHES

Several of Wyoming's best-known and most luxurious dude ranches are in Jackson Hole, providing wonderful places for families who are looking to rough it in style. Many more guest ranches are just over Togwotee Pass in the Dubois area and to the south in the Pinedale area. Grand Teton National Park has several of the most popular dude ranches, including:

- **Goosewing Ranch** (www.goosewingranch. com)
- **Gros Ventre River Ranch** (www.grosventreriverranch.com)
- **Heart Six Ranch** (www.heartsix.com)
- **Lost Creek Ranch** (www.lostcreek.com)
- **Moose Head Ranch** (www.ranchweb.com/ moose-head-ranch)
- **Red Rock Ranch** (www.theredrockranch. com)
- **Triangle X Ranch** (www.trianglex.com)
- **Turpin Meadow Ranch** (www.turpinmeadowranch.com)

Flat Creek Ranch

At the base of Sheep Mountain, Flat Creek Ranch (307/733-0603 or 866/522-3344, www. flatcreekranch.com) is packed with history. The land was originally homesteaded by cowboy, hunting guide, and rustler Cal Carrington, but he sold it to his close friend, "Countess" Cissy Patterson, in 1923. Previously married to a Polish count, Cissy came from a wealthy Chicago newspaper family, but her love of the West and horses matched Cal's. For two decades Cissy and Cal were grist for the gossip mill, mostly during her trips to Wyoming, but also when she took him along on a grand tour of Europe. Cissy died in 1948, and her relatives now own the ranch. After a long hiatus and

extensive improvements, this historic ranch in a gorgeous setting is once again open for guests, with five renovated cabins and three gourmet meals daily. The emphasis is on fly-fishing in legendary Flat Creek; the ranch owns 1.5 miles along the stream. Other activities include horseback rides and hikes into the Gros Ventre Wilderness, canoeing, and a wood-fired sauna for chilly evenings. There's a three-night minimum stay in the summer ($675 for two people per night, all-inclusive). The ranch is 15 miles up a bumpy dirt road, but the ranch provides transportation (Mon. and Fri. only) if you don't have a four-wheel-drive with high clearance. Open late May–late September.

R Lazy S Ranch

Another historic dude ranch is R Lazy S Ranch (near Teton Village along the Moose-Wilson Rd., 307/733-2655, www.rlazys.com), with space for 45 guests, who enjoy horseback rides, fishing, and other Western adventures. A one-week minimum stay is required. All-inclusive rates range widely depending upon the cabin: $2,745–4,032 for two people per week. Lazy S is open mid-June–September. Tykes under age seven are not allowed.

Spotted Horse Ranch

On the banks of the Hoback River, 16 miles south of Jackson, Spotted Horse Ranch (307/733-2097 or 800/528-2084, www.spottedhorseranch.com) exudes a comfortable rusticity. The main lodge and cabins contain lodgepole furniture, and a maximum of 35 guests stay in log cabins with modern conveniences. Activities include horseback riding (some Appaloosas), fly-fishing, cookouts, and river trips, and you can unwind in the hot tub or sauna. A one-week minimum stay is required in the summer ($4,500 d per week, all-inclusive). Open mid-May–October.

MOUNTAIN RESORTS

East of Moran Junction at Togwotee Pass (9,658 feet), U.S. Highway 26/287 tops the Continental Divide and then slides eastward toward Dubois and the Wind River Valley. The

Togwotee Pass area is famous for luxuriously deep snow all winter and is a destination for snowmobilers, cross-country skiers, and dog-sledding enthusiasts. Just north of the pass is Teton Wilderness, a place to discover what solitude means. As you face west from the pass, the Teton Range offers a jagged horizon line. This entire area provides a delicious escape from hectic Jackson and is home to two noteworthy, attractive high-elevation resorts: Togwotee Mountain Lodge and Brooks Lake Lodge.

Togwotee Mountain Lodge

Forty-eight miles northeast of Jackson and just a few miles west of Togwotee Pass is Togwotee Mountain Lodge (307/543-2847 or 800/543-2847, www.togwoteelodge.com), a pleasantly rustic place to spend a night or a week. Owned by the conglomerate Aramark, the resort offers horseback rides, and the staff can set up mountain-bike trips, whitewater rafting, fly-fishing, backcountry pack trips, and other summertime adventures, along with wintertime snowmobiling (the primary winter activity), dogsledding, and cross-country skiing when the snow flies. Togwotee has a variety of accommodations, and guests will enjoy two large hot tubs. Summer rates are $170 d for rooms in the lodge, $200 d for family rooms with bunk beds for the kids, and $230 d for one-bedroom cabins. The mini-suites and cabins sleep up to six people ($10 per person for more than two). In winter, the resort specializes in package deals that include lodging, breakfast and dinner, snowmobile guide, and free airport shuttle. The resort also houses a restaurant ($15–27), bar, gas station, gift shop, and convenience store. Togwotee is closed early April–mid-May and mid-October–November.

Brooks Lake Lodge

Brooks Lake Lodge (307/455-2121, www.brookslake.com) may have the finest location of any Wyoming resort, with a placid lake in front and the cliffs of Pinnacle Buttes nearby. Built in 1922, it has long served travelers en route to Yellowstone, and its enormous great hall contains big-game trophies from all over the world. Completely restored, the lodge is now on the National Register of Historic Places. Seven guest rooms are available in the main lodge, and eight attractive cabins hide in the trees; all are tastefully appointed with handmade lodgepole furniture. The cabins also have woodstoves.

The turnoff for Brooks Lake Lodge is 65 miles northeast of Jackson (34 miles east of Moran Junction) and another five miles off the highway via Brooks Lake Road. The lodge is open mid-June–mid-September and late December–mid-March. There's a three-night minimum stay, and rates are $650–750 per day for two guests in the lodge or cabins. The largest and most luxurious cabin has two bedrooms, a living room, kitchen, jetted tub, and more for $1,700 nightly. All rates include gourmet meals, horseback riding, guided hiking, canoeing, fly-fishing, and Wi-Fi in the summer. A stocked casting pond is available for working on your technique. The spa features a small workout room, sauna, and outdoor hot tub; massage and facials are extra. Winter stays include three meals, cross-country skis, ice-fishing, and snowshoes, plus spa access for $500–550 per day for two people (two-night minimum). Snowmobile rentals and dogsled tours are also available. Brooks Lake Lodge is open to the public for winter lunches (burgers, sandwiches, salads, and daily specials), making this a popular stop for snowmobilers and cross-country skiers.

RENTALS
Condominiums

Condominiums provide a popular option for families and groups visiting Jackson Hole. These privately owned places are maintained by several local property-management companies and vary from small studio apartments to spacious five-bedroom houses. All are completely furnished (including dishes) and have fireplaces, cable TV, phones, and mid-stay maid service if you remain more than five nights. The nicest also include access to pools and hot tubs and have balconies overlooking the spectacular Tetons. Many of the condominiums are in Teton Village (adjacent to the ski area) or a couple of miles south in Teton Pines or the Aspens; others are scattered around Jackson Hole, so make sure you get a place close to your interests.

Condo prices vary widely depending upon location and amenities, but during the winter holiday season (Christmas–early Jan.), expect to pay $190–230 per night for studio or one-bedroom condos (1–2 people). Two-bedroom units (up to four people) cost $280–320 per night, and full four-bedroom/three-bath condos (these sleep eight) run $375–520 per night. The most sumptuous places will set you back $4,800 nightly in the peak winter season, but if you're feeling flush with cash, rent one of the finest homes for a mere $28,000 a month! Summer and off-peak winter rates are often 35–50 percent lower, with spring and fall rates 50–70 percent lower than peak-season prices. In fall or spring, condos offer a real bargain for traveling families looking to stay several nights in the area. Minimum stays of 3–7 nights are required throughout the year, with the longest minimum stays required in the peak winter season.

If you have the luxury of time, do a little comparison shopping before renting a condo. Things to ask include whether you have access to a pool and hot tub, how close you are to the ski slopes, how frequent the maid service is, and whether the units include such amenities as Wi-Fi, DVD players, flat-screen TVs, washers, and dryers. Also be sure to find out what beds are in the rooms, because couples might not enjoy sleeping in twin bunk beds. Ask about the age and condition of the condos, since some are dated. The newest units are at Love Ridge (next to Snow King Resort) and White Buffalo Club (downtown). Fortunately, the rental companies provide helpful online photos, floor plans, and other details for the various styles of condos.

Contact the following companies for details:

- **Four Seasons Resort** (307/732-5000, www.fourseasons.com/jacksonhole)

- **Grand View Lodge & Spa** (at Snow King Resort, 307/733-3186 or 800/522-5464, www.grandviewlodgeandspa.com)

- **Jackson Hole Lodge** (307/733-2992 or 800/604-9404, www.jacksonholelodge.com)

- **Jackson Hole Reservations** (307/733-6331 or 800/329-9205, www.jacksonhole.net)

- **Jackson Hole Resort Lodging** (307/733-3990 or 800/443-8613, www.jhrl.com)

- **Love Ridge Resort Lodges** (at Snow King Resort, 307/733-5200 or 800/533-7669, www.loveridgelodge.com)

- **Mountain Property Management** (307/733-1684 or 800/992-9948, www.mpmjh.com)

- **OK Rentals** (307/733-8604 or 800/735-8310, www.jackson-hole-vacations.com)

- **Rendezvous Mountain Rentals** (307/739-9050 or 888/739-2565, www.rmrentals.com)

- **Snow King Resort Condominiums** (307/733-5200 or 800/522-5464, www.snowking.com)

- **Spring Creek Ranch** (307/733-8833 or 800/443-6139, www.springcreekranch.com)

- **Teton Pines Resort and Country Club** (307/733-1005 or 800/238-2223, www.tetonpines.com)

The largest of these businesses—and a good place to begin your search—is Jackson Hole Resort Lodging. Owned by Jackson Hole Mountain Resort, it manages about 200 places. Other large management companies include Rendezvous Mountain Rentals and Snow King Resort Condominiums. The last of these also owns (and can book condos at) Grand View Lodge & Spa and Love Ridge Resort Lodging.

Two resorts offer fractional-ownership condos in Jackson Hole: **The Residence Club at Teton Pines** (307/733-1005 or 800/238-2223, www.tetonpinesresidenceclub.com) and **The**

Teton Club (307/734-9777 or 866/352-9777, www.tetonclub.com). The Teton Club is right at the base of Jackson Hole Resort, making it perfect for skiers, while Teton Pines offers an upscale country club with a golf course and other amenities. Members typically share ownership and stay for 4–12 weeks per year. Also check out the **White Buffalo Club** (160 W. Gill Ave., 307/734-4900 or 888/256-8182, www.whitebuffaloclub.com), a member-only operation in the heart of Jackson.

Home Rentals and Swaps

Jackson Hole home rentals—both short- and long-term—are available from **Jackson Hole Reservations** (307/733-6331 or 800/329-9205, www.jacksonhole.net), **OK Rentals** (307/733-8604 or 800/735-8310, www.jackson-hole-vacations.com), **Mountain Property Management** (307/733-1684 or 800/992-9948, www.mpmjh.com), **Rendezvous Mountain Rentals** (307/739-9050 or 888/739-2565, www.rmrentals.com), **Mountain Haus** (307/690-1034, www.jhmountainhaus.com), and **Rocking-V Lodge** (307/733-7319, www.rocking-v.com).

Rancho Alegre Lodge (3600 S. Park Loop Rd., 307/733-7988, www.ranchoalegre.com) offers Jackson's most expensive lodging. On a 50-acre spread facing the Tetons, this 10,000-square-foot structure houses seven bedrooms (each with its own TV/VCR, phone, and fridge) and offers an upscale hunting lodge decor along with such amenities as concierge service, a private chef available for hire, seven fireplaces, extensive decks, a hot tub, and a pool table. Full-house rentals (up to 20 guests) are $2,600 per night, including continental breakfasts, with a four-night minimum stay in the summer (and four times $2,600 is $10,400…). At these prices, the lodge is primarily used for weddings, corporate retreats, large and wealthy families, and ski groups.

At the base of the mountains in Wilson, **Trail Creek Ranch** (307/733-2610, www.jacksonholetrailcreekranch.com) operated as a dude ranch for 50 years. Lodging on this 270-acre spread ranges from a double room with a king bed ($140; no kitchen) to a two-bedroom cabin ($270) with full kitchen that's perfect for friends. All units have private baths and limited Wi-Fi, but no distracting TVs. Families love the heated outdoor pool. Trail Creek is open June–September, with a three-day minimum stay.

In addition to the lodging places described, visitors to Jackson Hole may want to investigate a house exchange. Several online companies list homeowners in Jackson who are interested in a trade if you have an upscale home, especially one on the beach in midwinter! If you live in Hawaii or Costa Rica and want to go skiing, your home might be a hot property. If you live in North Dakota or Baghdad, good luck. Companies worth investigating include **Home Exchange** (310/798-3864 or 800/877-8723, www.homeexchange.com), **Home Link** (954/566-2687 or 800/638-3841, www.swapnow.com), and **Intervac** (415/839-9670 or 800/756-4663, www.intervac-homeexchange.com).

Another option is through one of the online vacation rental brokers, such as **Vacation Rentals by Owner** (www.vrbo.com), **CyberRentals** (www.cyberrentals.com), or **Vacation Homes** (www.vacationhomes.com).

Camping

Fully 97 percent of Jackson Hole is publicly owned, primarily within Grand Teton National Park and Bridger-Teton National Forest. So many options exist that campers can pitch their tent in a new campground every night for three weeks. Private RV parks are considerably more limited, but a half-dozen are scattered around the valley.

PUBLIC CAMPGROUNDS

Most public campgrounds on Forest Service and Park Service lands around Jackson Hole are on a first-come, first-camp basis with no reservations. In addition to these campsites, many people camp for free on dispersed sites on Forest Service lands; contact the agency for locations and restrictions.

Bridger-Teton Campgrounds

Bridger-Teton National Forest (307/739-5400, www.fs.fed.us/r4/btnf) has a number of campgrounds ($10–15; open mid-May–Sept.) located around Jackson Hole. Closest is **Curtis Canyon Campground,** seven miles northeast of Jackson up a gravel road with a fine view of the Tetons.

Three popular Bridger-Teton campgrounds are southwest of Jackson in the Snake River Canyon, with access via U.S. Highway 26/89. They include **East Table Creek Campground** and **Station Creek Campground,** both 24 miles south of Jackson and 11 miles southwest of Hoback Junction, along with **Wolf Creek Campground,** 26 miles southwest of Jackson and six miles from Hoback Junction.

Three more campgrounds are northeast of Jackson in the Gros Ventre Valley. **Atherton Creek Campground** sits along Slide Lake, 18 miles northeast of Jackson and seven miles northeast of Kelly up Gros Ventre Road. **Red Hills Campground** and **Crystal Creek Campground** are near each other along the Gros Ventre River, approximately 23 miles northeast of Jackson and 13 miles up the partly gravel Gros Ventre Road.

In the Buffalo Valley area 45 miles northeast of Jackson, pitch your tent at **Hatchet Campground,** eight miles east of Moran Junction; **Turpin Meadow Campground,** 10 miles east of Moran Junction; or **Box Creek Campground,** along Buffalo Valley Road.

Forty-nine miles north of Jackson, **Angles Campground** is a small site just uphill from Togwotee Mountain Resort on U.S. Highway 287. Another small camping place, **Sheffield Creek Campground,** 55 miles north of Jackson, is off U.S. Highway 89/191/287 near Flagg Ranch Resort (poor road access until late summer). Remote **Pacific Creek Campground** is 46 miles north of Jackson and nine miles up Pacific Creek Road, with access through Grand Teton National Park.

Two campgrounds are approximately 20 miles southeast of Jackson along the Hoback River: **Kozy Campground,** seven miles southeast of Hoback Junction, and **Hoback Campground,** eight miles east of Hoback Junction.

Close to Granite Hot Springs—a delightful place for a soak—**Granite Campground** is 35 miles southeast of Jackson and nine miles up the gravel Granite Creek Road.

Caribou-Targhee Campgrounds

Trail Creek Campground and **Mike Harris Campground** are in the **Caribou-Targhee National Forest** (208/354-2312, www.fs.fed.us/r4/caribou-targhee, $10) on the west side of Teton Pass, approximately 20 miles west of Jackson. Both are open mid-May–mid-September, with reservations ($9 fee) available at 518/885-3639 or 877/444-6777, www.recreation.gov.

RV PARKS

As land values have soared, the number of RV parks in Jackson has dropped. Today, only two RV resorts remain, with two more a dozen miles to the south and three more north of town in or near Grand Teton National Park.

The private RV parks around Jackson can be surprisingly expensive: Some places charge more for a tent space than it would cost to stay in a motel room in many Wyoming towns! Even more expensive is a ticket for parking RVs overnight on Jackson city streets. It's illegal to do so, and police strictly enforce the ordinance.

On the south end of town behind the Virginian Lodge, **Virginian RV Park** (750 W. Broadway Ave., 307/733-7189 or 800/321-6982 in summer or 800/262-4999 in winter, www.virginianlodge.com) is the biggest RV parking lot in the area. Full hookups at more than 100 sites (many pull-through spaces) cost $65; no tents. Guests at the RV park can use the Virginian Lodge's outdoor pool and hot tub. Wi-Fi is available in the hotel lobby. The park is open May–mid-October.

The best local option—by far—is **Jackson Hole Campground** (2780 N. Moose-Wilson Rd., 307/413-0495, www.jacksonholecampground. com, $35 tents, $65 RVs, open year-round), with a quiet, shady location near Calico Restaurant on the road to Teton Village. There's a shower house, cable TV, Wi-Fi, and a camp store, but no laundry. Call ahead for reservations.

Two private campgrounds are in the Hoback Junction area, 12 miles south of Jackson. **Lazy J Corral** (307/733-1554) is right on the highway at Hoback Junction, but the rates are low: RV sites with full hookups cost just $27. It does not have tent spaces but is open year-round.

Snake River Park KOA (307/733-7078 or 800/562-1878, www.snakeriverpark.com), 12 miles south of Jackson at Hoback Junction, has RV spaces for $43–59 d, tent sites for $38 d, and simple "kamping kabins" for $77–89 d. It's open early April–November. The KOA has a riverside location and a game room. Snake River Park Whitewater rafting company is also based here.

Food

Jackson stands out from the rest of Wyoming on the culinary scene: Chicken-fried steak may be available, but it certainly isn't the house specialty! You won't need to look far to find good food; in fact, the town seems to overflow with memorable (and even more memorably priced) eateries. If you stood in Town Square and walked in any direction for a block, you would find at least one restaurant that would be a standout in any other Wyoming town. More than 70 local restaurants do business here—in a town that contains just 9,000 people.

To get an idea of what to expect at local restaurants, pick up a copy of the free *Jackson Hole Dining Guide* at the visitor center, local restaurants, or online (www.focusproductions. com). The guide includes sample menus and brief descriptions of many local establishments. All local restaurants are now entirely smoke-free.

BREAKFAST

The best breakfast place in Jackson isn't in Jackson, but in Wilson, where **Nora's Fish Creek Inn** (307/733-8288, 6:30 A.M.–2 P.M. and 5:30–9 P.M. Mon.–Fri., 6:30 A.M.–1:30 P.M. and 5:30–9 P.M. Sat.–Sun., $19–28) attracts a full house each morning. The food (including *huevos rancheros,* biscuits and gravy, and omelets) is great, the setting is authentically rustic, and the waitresses are friendly and fast. Nora's also serves tried-and-true lunches and dinners at fair prices, from patty melts ($7) to nut-crusted halibut ($25). Dinner reservations required in the summer.

A longtime morning standout is **The Bunnery** (130 N. Cache Dr., 307/733-5474 or 800/349-0492, www.bunnery.com, daily 7 A.M.–9 P.M. in summer, till 7 P.M. in winter, $7–10), with good omelets and fresh-squeezed juices, plus delicious sandwiches on freshly baked breads, salads, burgers, homemade soups, and espresso. There's plenty of space inside, with a patio deck for summer mornings. The Bunnery bakes a variety of pies, cakes, and other sweets, but it's best known for hearty-flavored OSM (oat, sunflower, and millet) bread—on the pricey side at almost $6 a loaf.

Teton Steakhouse (40 W. Pearl St., 307/733-2639, www.tetonsteakhouse.com, daily 6:30 A.M.–11 P.M.) serves a two-notches-on-your-belt breakfast buffet ($7), with pancakes, bacon, sausage, potatoes, fruits, and more (coffee and juice are extra).

Bubba's Bar-B-Que Restaurant (100 Blackcreek Dr., 307/733-2288, daily 6:30 A.M.–10 P.M. in summer, daily 6:30 A.M.–8:30 P.M. in winter, $5–9) is another cheap and tasty option, with a very filling worker's special ($7). Ask for it, since you won't find it on the menu.

In Teton Village, head downstairs at the Mangy Moose to **RMO Café** (307/734-9438, www.mangymoose.net, daily 7 A.M.–5 P.M., $5–8), offering killer breakfasts along with inexpensive burgers, pizza-by-the-slice ($3), and sandwiches, salads, and burgers for lunch.

E. Leaven Food Co. (175 N. Center St., 307/733-5600, www.eleavenfood.com, daily 7 A.M.–3 P.M. in summer, 8 A.M.–3 P.M. in winter, $6–9) has a bright location a block off the Square. Take a table beside the tall windows facing the leafy alley. Breakfast omelets, quiche, bagels, Belgian waffles, and monster cinnamon rolls are followed by lunchtime hot and cold sandwiches and salads. There's good espresso and box lunches, too.

COFFEE AND SWEETS

Housed in a tiny log cabin a block off the Square, **Shades Café** (25 S. King St., 307/733-2015, www.facebook.com, daily 7:30 A.M.–3 P.M.) has a shady summer-only side patio. Breakfasts feature eggs Benedict (recommended), muesli, and fresh-baked croissants, plus lattes, mochas, and other coffee drinks. Lunch standouts are salads, quiches, burritos, and panini. Shades is a relaxing place to hang out with the espresso habitués, although it does close early in the fall, winter, and spring.

Just off Town Square, **Jackson Hole Roasters** (145 E. Broadway Ave., 307/690-9318, www.jacksonholeroasters.com, 7 A.M.–7 P.M. Mon.–Fri., 8 A.M.–7 P.M. Sat.–Sun.) roasts organic, fair-trade coffees. Get a pound to go or have the barista craft an espresso *doppio* on their hi-tech Clover machine.

🅲 **Atelier Ortega** (150 Scott Ln., 307/734-6400, www.atelierortega.com, 8 A.M.–8 P.M. Mon.–Sat., 9 A.M.–5 P.M. Sun.) is the creation of Mexican-born Oscar Ortega, a master pastry chef whose accolades include numerous international awards. Crème brûlée, truffles, and other luscious confections await true chocoholics. These are heavenly works of art, almost too perfect to eat.

LUNCH

One of the most popular noontime spots in Jackson—it's been here more than 35 years—is **Sweetwater Restaurant** (85 King St., 307/733-3553, www.sweetwaterjackson.com, daily 11:30 A.M.–3 P.M. and 5:30–10 P.M. in summer, 11:30 A.M.–3 P.M. and 5:30–9 P.M. in winter, $18–24). The historic log cabin has several tables on the front deck and a lunch menu ($10–12) of dependably good salads, homemade soups, and earthy sandwiches. For dinner, try cedar-plank wild salmon, elk osso bucco, or chicken-fried pork.

Better known as DOG, 🅲 **Down on Glen** (307/733-4422, daily 7 A.M.–2 P.M., 5:30–10 P.M. Fri.–Sun.) is a minuscule eatery next to Mountain High Pizza at Glenwood and Broadway with a schizophrenic personality. Locals—and in-the-know tourists—crowd in for tasty and cheap breakfast burritos (just $6), organic buffalo burgers, and Philly cheesesteaks early in the day. Owner Sange Sherpa's roots emerge weekend evenings, when DOG becomes **Everest Momo Shack,** serving Nepalese specialties ($10–13), including curry dishes, tikka masala, and momo dumplings, all with a side of naan bread. Delicious, but because everything is freshly made you'll need to wait—and sometimes quite a while. Primarily a to-go spot, DOG has a couple of picnic tables on the patio. Breakfast and lunch are served year-round, but Nepalese meals are available only in summer and winter.

A popular hole-in-the-wall just off the Square, **Backcountry Provisions** (50 W. Deloney St., 307/734-9420, www.backcountryprovisions.com, daily 7 A.M.–5 P.M., $7–8) creates tasty, healthy sandwiches. Try the Dolomite, with prosciutto, salami, provolone, red peppers, and red onion.

Betty Rock Café (325 W. Pearl, 307/733-0747, www.bettyrock.com, 10 A.M.–5 P.M. Mon.–Sat., till 10 P.M. Thurs., $7–9) is a great and noisy place for brunch, with delectable homemade breads, breakfast egg sandwiches, pastrami melts, turkey havarti panini, Thai wraps, salads, soups, and espresso. Drop by on Thursday nights for all-you-can-eat gourmet pizzas ($11, add $4 for Caesar salad). The waitstaff brings out different pizza variations throughout the evening.

A peaceful side-street location, an eclectic all-organic menu with vegan options, and fresh baked goods are all attractions for **Lotus Café** (145 N. Glenwood St., 307/734-0882, www.tetonlotuscafe.com, daily 7 A.M.–7 P.M. in summer, 8 A.M.–9:30 P.M. in winter, $6–11 breakfast and lunch, $13–22 dinner). The menu sprawls across an array of dishes and cuisines, from cinnamon French toast to coconut cashew *biryani*. Fresh-squeezed juices, espresso, and free Wi-Fi are available.

Off the beaten track in Wilson, 🅒 **Chippy's Kitchen** (307/690-3214, www.jacksonholecatering.com, daily 11:30 A.M.–6 P.M.) is a hidden gem. Owner/chef Chippy Sherman also operates a popular catering business. The tiny cabin gets slammed for lunch, with enormous sandwiches ($8–9) made from whatever is fresh in the kitchen—creations like jalapeño-cheddar corn bread with prosciutto, brie, and roasted asparagus. Daily specials feature soups, salads, and amazing desserts (try the ice-cream sandwich cookies). Check the cooler for dinners to go ($10–15). Closed mid-October–mid-November and mid-April–mid-May.

Find delicious sub sandwiches on tangy homemade bread at **New York City Sub Shop** (20 N. Jackson St., 307/733-4414, www.newyorkcitysubshop.com, 10 A.M.–7 P.M. Mon.–Fri., 10 A.M.–6 P.M. Sat., 10 A.M.–5 P.M. Sun. in summer, reduced hours in winter). It's a little pricey ($7 for a half hoagie or $12 for a whole), but the service is fast, and the hot sandwiches are vastly better than the Subway versions.

Pearl Street Bagels (145 Pearl St., 307/739-1218, daily 6:30 A.M.–6 P.M.) serves home-baked bagels on the small side, along with good espresso and juices. There's a second Pearl Street over in Wilson (307/739-1261); it's *the* groovy place to be seen in Wilson (okay, so are Nora's, Chippy's, and the 'Coach).

For lunches in the Teton Village area, stop by **Westside Store and Deli** (307/733-6202, daily 7 A.M.–9 P.M.) in the Aspens. The deli will be glad to pack you a big picnic lunch, and it also sells entrées (about $6) such as lemon-Dijon chicken, lasagna, and ribs.

The National Museum of Wildlife Art, two miles north of Jackson on U.S. Highway 26/89, houses a bright little restaurant with windows facing the National Elk Refuge. The **Rising Sage Café** (307/733-8649, www.risingsagecafe.com, daily 11 A.M.–3 P.M., $6–11) has a lunch menu of sandwiches (try the chicken salad croissant), buffalo burgers, homemade soups, chili, salads, and espresso.

AMERICAN

Jackson's most popular family eatery is 🅒 **Bubba's Bar-B-Que Restaurant** (100 Blackcreek Dr., 307/733-2288, daily 6:30 A.M.–10 P.M. in summer, 6:30 A.M.–8:30 P.M. in winter, $13–20). Each evening the parking lot out front is jammed with folks waiting patiently for a chance to gnaw on barbecued spare ribs, savor the spicy chicken wings, or gobble up the turkey plate. Get here before 6:30 P.M. for shorter lines at the big salad bar ($8). Lunch is a real bargain with great specials ($8). Drinks, including beer and wine, come in recycled Mason jars. There are cheap and tasty breakfasts, too.

Get great all-American burgers at the 1950s-style **Billy's Burgers** (55 N. Cache Dr., 307/733-3279, www.cadillac-grille.com, daily

11:30 A.M.–10:30 P.M.), adjacent to the more upscale Cadillac Grille. The Billy burger ($6) is a half-pound monster.

Next door to Billy's and in the basement of the bar of the same name, the **Million Dollar Cowboy Steakhouse** (307/733-4790, www.cowboysteakhouse.net, daily 5:30–10 P.M.) specializes in "casual Western elegance" and great steaks, from sirloin to filet mignon. In addition, the menu encompasses salads, shrimp scampi, pasta, ribs, and a few lonesome vegetarian specials. The bar offers a dozen different single-malt scotches, plus seasonal drink specials. The Steakhouse is not for kids and it's not cheap: steaks are $26–48. Reservations are advised.

Also recommended is **Gun Barrel Steakhouse** (862 W. Broadway Ave., 307/733-3287, www.gunbarrel.com, daily 5:30–10 P.M., closed in Nov.), where the meaty mesquite-grilled steaks, elk, and buffalo are served in a delightful hunting-lodge atmosphere with trophy game mounts; they came from a wildlife museum that previously occupied the site. You'll find lots of historic guns and other Old West paraphernalia around the Gun Barrel too, making this an interesting place to explore even if you aren't hungry. Gun Barrel is a bit on the pricey side, with entrées for $17–37. The bar has a wide choice of beers on draught.

Very popular with both locals and ski bums is famous **Mangy Moose Restaurant & Saloon** (Teton Village, 307/733-4913, www.mangymoose.net, daily 11 A.M.–10 P.M. for food, drinks till 2 A.M., $15–24). The menu changes weekly, but typically includes sirloin steak, black Angus prime rib, Alaskan halibut, and Idaho rainbow trout. Sprawling over two levels, it's a fun and lively place. There's free Wi-Fi, and live bands play several nights a week year-round.

The menu and setting at **Teton Steakhouse** (40 W. Pearl St., 307/733-2639, 6:30 A.M.–10 P.M. Sun.–Thurs., 6:30 A.M.–11 P.M. Fri.–Sat.) reflect this restaurant's previous incarnation as a Sizzler, but that doesn't faze anyone. The central location (one block off Town Square), stuff-yourself meals, and noisy,

kid-friendly setting bring a crowd every day, even if the food is nothing special. Line up to put in your order for steaks ($17–30), ribs, or chicken, or just sidle up to the big salad, soup, and dessert bar to fill your plate. There also is a breakfast buffet and free Wi-Fi. This place is very popular with hogs who park their Hogs (Harleys) and waddle in, along with swarms of motorcoach tourists.

Next to Albertson's on the south end of Jackson, **Rendezvous Bistro** (380 South U.S. Hwy. 89, 307/739-1100, www.rendezvousbistro.net, daily 5:30–11 P.M. in summer, closed Sun. in winter, $17–32) has a strong local following for all-better-than-mom's meatloaf, Jamaican jerked chicken, veal marsala, duck confit, and a rather pricey oyster bar. Definitely recommended.

ASIAN
Chinese

In Grand Teton Plaza on the south end of town, **Chinatown Restaurant** (850 W. Broadway Ave., 307/733-8856, 11 A.M.–9:30 P.M. Mon.–Fri., 5–10 P.M. Sat., 5–9:30 P.M. Sun., $9–14) serves good Chinese dishes—particularly the *mu shu* vegetables, lemon chicken, and pot stickers—and offers weekday lunch specials ($8).

Ocean City China Bistro (340 W. Broadway Ave., 307/734-9768, daily 11 A.M.–9:30 P.M., $9–13) provides a pleasant downtown setting and more than 120 choices—from honey walnut prawns with pork to Szechwan Three Delight. Weekday lunch combo plates ($8) are a bargain.

Hong Kong Buffet (826 W. Broadway Ave., 307/734-8988, 10 A.M.–10:30 P.M. Mon.–Sat., 11 A.M.–10 P.M. Sun.) has an enormous 50-item buffet: $8 at lunch or $12 for dinner and all day Sunday.

Japanese

Get delicious freshly rolled sushi—including vegetarian rolls and a unique hot spicy tuna roll—at **Masa Sushi** (307/733-2962, 6–10 P.M. Tue.–Sun., $18–25), located inside The Inn at Jackson Hole in Teton Village. The setting is intimate and inviting.

Long a favorite with locals and visitors, **Nikai Sushi** (225 N. Cache, 307/734-6490, www.nikaisushi.com, daily 6–9:30 P.M.) serves creatively prepared sushi as the main attraction, but also has a menu of Asian fusion items from the open kitchen, including miso-glazed black cod, coconut fried chicken, and *wakame* seaweed salad. The atmosphere is contemporary and stylish. Most items are priced $10–20, but you'll also find $6 rolls. Reservations are advised.

Housed within the Jackson Hole Wine Company, **Koshu Wine Bar** (200 W. Broadway Ave., 307/733-5283, www.koshuwinebar.com, daily 5:30–10 P.M., $10–32) serves pan-Asian cuisine nightly in a tiny but classy setting with a big summer-only covered deck. The menu changes often, but typically includes butter chicken, Thai beef salad, and Korean-style ribs. You can choose from more than a dozen wines by the glass, or buy a bottle from the shop's extensive selection (corkage fee). A DJ spins tunes Thursday and Saturday nights till 2 A.M.

Thai

In an alley across the street from Teton Theater, friendly ◖ **Teton Thai Restaurant** (135 N. Cache Dr., 307/733-0022, www.tetonthai.com, 11:30 A.M.–3 P.M. and 5:30–10 P.M. Mon.–Sat., $14–18) is a favorite spot for 20-something locals. Pick a rice, noodle, or curry dish and add your choice of chicken, beef, shrimp, or tofu. Vegan and gluten-free options are available. Service can be haphazard and it may take time to get served, but you'll be glad you waited. All seating is outdoors, though some is under a deck. The festive atmosphere amps up on Thursday and Friday evenings when a DJ spins tunes till 11 P.M. Everything moves inside the tiny eatery when winter comes, with customers crowding into a handful of stools along the counter. No credit cards or alcohol, but it's fine to BYOB.

Thai Me Up Restaurant & Brewery (75 E. Pearl St., 307/733-0005, www.thaijh.com, daily 11:30 A.M.–11:30 P.M., $14–17) has a gimmicky name and a U.S.-born chef, but the food is spicy, creative, and delicious. It has a few sidewalk tables, plus a tiny bar with offbeat drinks, including the Bigglesworth Typhoon, a blow-me-down 45-ounce blend of seven different alcohols that's set afire. The location is a bit quieter than places on the Square. Entrées include a good choice of vegetarian and gluten-free dishes. G-13, wide noodles in a coconut kaffir curry, is a not-too-spicy favorite. The bottle beer list features many unique European beers; you can also try several beers brewed on the premises, including Thai Me Up 2x4 Quadruple Pale Ale.

ITALIAN

Hidden away on the north end of town next to Anvil Motel, **Nani's Cucina Italiana** (242 N. Glenwood, 307/733-3888, www.nanis.com, daily 5–10 P.M., $19–25) is a longtime favorite. Flowers cover the exterior in summer, and inside it's quiet and romantic. In addition to the standards, Nani's features a menu of specialties from a different region of Italy each month. The wine bar (Enoteca Sicula) has an extensive choice of Italian and California vintages. Patio dining is available in the summer. Reservations are recommended.

Owned by acclaimed chef Roger Freedman—formerly of Snake River Grill— ◖ **Il Villagio Osteria** (307/739-4100, www.jhosteria.com, daily noon–2 P.M. and 5:30–10 P.M., $18–34) is housed within Teton Village's luxurious Hotel Terra. It specializes in Italian cuisine, including house-made gnocchi, asparagus ravioli, and wonderful pizzas ($18) and panini from the wood-fired oven. The 12-seat wine bar is less formal, with plenty of Italian wines available by the glass or bottle. There's also a big outside deck facing the Teton Village fun. Reservations are essential.

Several other pizza places stand out in Jackson. You'll find **Calico Italian Restaurant & Bar** (307/733-2460, www.calicorestaurant.com, daily 5–10 P.M. restaurant, 5 P.M.–midnight bar) in the garish red-and-white building 0.75 mile north on Teton Village Road. The menu has gone a bit upscale, but prices are still manageable: $14–26 entrées, including such faves as linguini with spinach and chicken or Italian sausage lasagna from the open kitchen. A 12-inch personal pizza is $12. The bar at Calico is a locals' watering hole, and kids love the two-acre lawn/playground, wraparound covered porch, and flower-bedecked patio affording Teton vistas. START buses stop right out front, making this an easy destination even if you're without a car.

Mountain High Pizza Pie (120 W. Broadway Ave., 307/733-3646, www.mhpizza.com, daily 11 A.M.–11 P.M. in summer, till 10 P.M. in winter, $16) is a convenient tried-and-true downtown place offering all the usual toppings (and some not so, such as the Thai pie), plus calzones, subs, salads, and delivery to Jackson and Teton Village.

MEXICAN

For the fastest Mexican food in town (with the possible exception of Taco Bell), drop by **Pica's Mexican Taqueria** (1160 Alpine La., 307/734-4457, www.picastaqueria.com, daily 11 A.M.–10 P.M., $7–15). You'll find tasty tacos, bodacious burritos, enchanting enchiladas, and tempting *tortas* in a hip setting packed with locals. There's also a morning menu of breakfast burritos, huevos rancheros, and more on weekends. The shop is in the Buffalo Junction strip mall near Albertson's, with a second one inside Stagecoach Bar in Wilson.

In business since 1969, **The Merry Piglets** (160 N. Cache Dr., 307/733-2966, www.merrypiglets.com, daily 11:30 A.M.–10 P.M. in summer, 11:30 A.M.–9 P.M. in winter, $11–20) is a very busy place with a heart-of-town location. The menu features Tex-Mex meals, carne asada, fajitas, enchiladas, quesadillas, fish tacos, nachos, and cheese crisps—the house specialty. Excellent margaritas, pitchers of beer, and a skylit front section add to the appeal. Reservations are not accepted, so you'll find a long wait on midsummer evenings.

For a side of Jackson most tourists don't see, drop by **Alameda Tienda Mexicana** (975 Alpine Ave.) for Mexican pastries, meats, specialty groceries, and piñatas. The shop is hidden away in a tiny backstreet location.

FINE DINING

If you want fine continental dining and aren't deterred by entrées costing $25 or more, Jackson has much to offer.

Just off Town Square, **Snake River Grill** (upstairs at 84 E. Broadway Ave., 307/733-0557, www.snakerivergrill.com, daily 6:30–10 P.M.) is one of Jackson's finest gourmet restaurants—with prices to match ($21–42 entrées). Meals are exquisite, and the seasonal menu typically contains a variety of artfully presented seafood, free-range beef, and organic vegetables. The wine list is equally impressive, and there's a big rooftop deck (late June–Sept.) for alfresco dining on warm evenings. Reservations are a must; reserve two weeks in advance for prime-time seatings in the summer. Snake River Grill is a good place to scan for Jackson's best-known residents, Harrison Ford and Calista Flockhart. Closed November and April.

For views so spectacular they make it difficult to concentrate on your meal, don't miss **The Granary Restaurant** (307/732-8112, www.springcreekranch.com, daily 7–11 A.M., noon–2 P.M., and 5–9 P.M., closed Sun.–Tues. mid-Oct.–mid-Dec., $22–40), atop East Gros Ventre Butte west of Jackson with tall windows opening to the Tetons. This is also a great place for evening cocktails and romantic dining. Entrées include Idaho trout, Kobe beef sirloin steak, and a popular Cajun-spiced elk tenderloin. The separate lounge menu has lighter fare, including happy-hour specials 4–7 P.M. nightly, jazz on Friday, and a piano bar Saturday evenings.

Jackson's popular nouvelle cuisine restaurant— **C Cadillac Grille** (55 N. Cache on the square, 307/733-3279, www.cadillac-grille.com, daily 11:30 A.M.–3 P.M. and 5:30–10 P.M., $14–34)—serves creative meals, with a changing menu of seafood, filet mignon, buffalo burgers, and wild game. The art deco decor of the Cadillac helps make it one of the most crowded tourist hangouts in town, but it also attracts a devoted following of locals, especially during the nightly happy hour when two-for-one drinks are the draw. The restaurant includes a bar with lighter fare ($7–10 salads, ribs, and chicken wings), Billy's Burgers, and a covered rear patio for summertime dining.

Owned by a trio of local chefs, **Trio, An American Bistro** (45 S. Glenwood, 307/734-8038, www.bistrotrio.com, daily 11:30 A.M.–2:30 P.M. and 5:30–9 P.M.) is a trendy downtown eatery with high ceilings and a metallic decor. Start with sautéed mussels or arugula salad. House specialties include Tuscan grilled New York steak, wood-fired half chickens, and buffalo burgers. Be sure to order a side of their famous waffle fries with bleu cheese fondue. Most entrées are $15–30, but $12 will get you a simple mozzarella, marinara, and basil pizza. Reservations are advised.

Housed within Rusty Parrot Lodge, the acclaimed (**Wild Sage Restaurant** (175 N. Jackson, 307/733-2000 or 888/739-1749, www.rustyparrot.com, daily 5:30–9:30 P.M., $33–45) serves gourmet dinners in an intimate setting (just 26 seats). One of two AAA four-diamond restaurants in Jackson Hole, Wild Sage offers a delectable array of regional cuisine and fresh seafood. The menu changes, but typically includes pan-seared beef tenderloin, herb-crusted bison rib-eye, and ginger and citron crème brûlée, plus a fine choice of wines by the glass or bottle. Reservations are required; call a month ahead in midsummer. Breakfast (7–10 A.M.) is primarily for lodge guests, but is open to the public when space is available (more common in winter). The morning menu has several options, from a granola, yogurt, fruit, pastry, and coffee bar ($7) up to an all-you-can-eat spread ($15).

Located atop Bridger gondola at Jackson Hole Resort, (**Couloir Restaurant** (307/739-2675, www.couloirrestaurant.com) has gained accolades from both Condé Nast and *Food and Wine*. This special-occasion spot features views of Corbet's Couloir and the valley of Jackson Hole 2,800 feet below, with four-course dinners for $85 per person ($145 with paired wines). Signature dishes include an amazing house-smoked tenderloin of buffalo and a "locavore" salad from farmers' market vegetables and fruits. Desserts and cocktails

are equally notable. The setting is contemporary, and dinner reservations are highly recommended (available at www.opentable.com). The gondola (free in summer, free for restaurant patrons only in winter) starts running at 4:30 P.M. The vistas from the big outside patio (The Deck) are especially pretty at sunset; a bar menu features appetizers, sliders, burgers, shared plates, and happy-hour specials. Summer hours for both Couloir and The Deck are 5–11 P.M. Sunday–Friday late June–early September (closed Sat.). The Deck closes for winter, but Headwall Deli opens for ski season downstairs from Couloir. During ski season, Couloir is open 5:45–10 P.M. Friday–Saturday and daily for lunch.

BREWERIES

Before Prohibition in 1920, nearly every town in Wyoming had its own brewery, making such local favorites as Hillcrest, Schoenhofen, and Sweetwater. After repeal of "the noble experiment," breweries again popped up, but competition from industrial giants such as Anheuser-Busch and Coors forced the last Wyoming operation—Sheridan Brewing—out of business in 1954. It was another 34 years before commercial beer-making returned. In 1988, Charlie Otto started a tiny backyard operation in Wilson. His **Grand Teton Brewing Company** (208/787-4000 or 888/899-1656, www.grandtetonbrewing.com) brews just over Teton Pass in Victor, Idaho, where you can sample Teton Ale, Old Faithful Ale, Howling Wolf Weisse Bier, Bitch Creek ESB, and Sweetgrass IPA. You'll find them on tap at many Jackson-area bars and restaurants and for sale in six-pack bottles throughout the region.

An old warehouse two blocks from Town Square has been beautifully transformed into (**Snake River Brewing Co. and Restaurant** (265 S. Millward St., 307/739-2337, www.snakeriverbrewing.com, daily 11:30 A.M.–2 A.M., food served till 11 P.M.). The bright, cavernous setting fills with a convivial—and very loud—crowd of young

© DON PITCHER

Snake River Brewing Co. and Restaurant

outdoors enthusiasts most evenings, and the bar generally has seven or eight of their award-winning beers on tap, along with 40 or so from other brewers. Particularly notable—they've all won gold medals at many international brew festivals—are Zonker Stout, A.K. Session, and Snake River Pale Ale. The lunch and dinner café menu includes delicious thin-crust pizzas baked in the apple-wood–fired oven, flavorful appetizers, daily pasta specials, half-pound burgers, panini sandwiches, and salads. This is great food in a lively atmosphere, and one of *the* places to be seen in Jackson. Most entrées run $9–15, but the brewery also serves a number of $7 lunch specials. While this is a brewpub, it's also completely family friendly, with a kids' menu and so much background noise nobody will know when the baby starts screaming. Happy-hour (4–6 P.M.) beers are just $2.50, and you can add a big homemade soft pretzel for another buck or tasty chicken wings for a few more. There's free Wi-Fi, too.

WINE SHOPS

The most complete local wine and beer shops are **Westside Wine and Spirits** (307/733-5038) in the Aspens along Teton Village Road, **The Liquor Store** (next to Albertson's on W. Broadway Ave., 307/733-4466, www.wineliquorbeer.com), and **Dornan's Wine Shoppe** (307/733-2415, ext. 202, www.dornans.com) in Moose. The Liquor Store features an impressive upstairs wine department, plus a wine bar with free tastings of a half-dozen wines Fridays 4–7 P.M. **Jackson Hole Wine Company** (200 W. Broadway Ave., 307/739-9463, www.jacksonholewinecompany.com) also has a fine selection, with Koshu Wine Bar in the back.

GROCERIES AND NATURAL FOODS

Get groceries from the large **Albertson's** (307/733-5950, www.albertsons.com) on the south end of town at the corner of Buffalo Way and Broadway Avenue. Inside you'll find a bakery, pharmacy, deli, one-hour photo lab, bank branch, and coffee bar. This is the most lucrative Albertson's in the entire chain of 2,300 stores; sales are said to be three times higher than the second-most-successful store! A few blocks farther south (right in front of the high school) is an even larger **Smith's** (1425 S. U.S. Hwy. 89, 307/733-8908, www.smithsfoodanddrug.com), with the same features as Albertson's and a deli serving fresh sushi.

In Powderhorn Mall, **Jackson Whole Grocer** (974 W. Broadway Ave., 307/733-0450, www.jacksonwholegrocer.com, daily 7 A.M.–11 P.M.) is a hybrid of sorts between an organic grocer and a traditional supermarket. The emphasis is upon fresh and local items, but there's also a great bakery, full deli, fresh-squeezed juices, and espresso.

The popular **Jackson Hole Farmers Market** (www.jacksonholefarmersmarket.org) comes to Town Square Saturdays 8–11 A.M. July–mid-September. Shop for fresh veggies, fruits, food, and flowers. Live music and cooking demonstrations add to the attraction. A separate **People's Market** (307/690-0705, www.jhpeoplesmarket.org) takes place on Wednesday 4–7 P.M. at the Lutheran Church on the corner of Gill and Willow Streets.

In business since 1947, **Jackson Hole** **Buffalo Meat Company** (1325 S. Hwy. 89, 307/733-4159 or 800/543-6328, www.jhbuffalomeat.com) sells smoked buffalo salami, jerky, sausage, steaks, and burgers, along with buffalo meat gift packs and elk steaks. It's in the Smith's mall.

Getting There and Around

Access to Jackson Hole has become easier in recent years, with several airlines and daily buses now serving the valley. Most summer visitors arrive by car, although a few more adventurous souls pedal in on bikes. If you're looking for or offering a ride, KMTN (96.9 FM, 307/733-4500, www.kmtnthemountain.com) has daily ride-finder announcements during its Trash and Treasure radio program. Tune in weekdays 9:30–9:50 A.M.

Several local travel agencies offer reservation services for those who prefer to leave the planning to someone else. They can set up airline tickets, rental cars, lodging, horseback riding, fishing trips, whitewater rafting, ski vacations, and all sorts of other packages. The biggest is the long-established **Jackson Hole Central Reservations** (307/733-4005 or 800/443-6931, www.jacksonholewy.com), which produces a slick glossy publication of featured properties. **Jackson Hole Reservations** (307/733-6331 or 800/329-9205, www.jacksonhole.net) has an equally complete listing of local places.

BY AIR

Jackson Hole Airport (307/733-7682, www.jacksonholeairport.com) is eight miles north of Jackson inside Grand Teton National Park. The remodeled airport is small and cozy but offers daily jet service to several U.S. cities. It's the only commercial airport within any national park, and the Grand Teton Association maintains a gift shop here. Stop by the **Ground Transportation Information Desk** (open daily 9 A.M.–5 P.M. year-round) for helpful maps and advice. Nearby are courtesy phones for local businesses and racks of brochures. You'll also find free Wi-Fi and a restaurant.

Delta/SkyWest (800/221-1212, www.delta.com) has year-round flights from Salt Lake City, with summer and winter service from Minneapolis/St. Paul and Atlanta. **American** (800/433-7300, www.aa.com) has summer and winter flights to Dallas and Chicago. **United/United Express** (800/864-8331, www.united.com) offers year-round service from Denver and Chicago, plus summertime flights out of Los Angeles. **Frontier Airlines** (800/432-1359, www.frontierairlines.com) has summer-only flights from Denver; these are turboprops, not jets. (Some Delta/SkyWest and United/United Express flights from Denver and Salt Lake City are also on these smaller planes.) In addition, the tarmac is often crowded with Lear and Gulfstream jets and other noisy transportation symbols of the elite.

Amazingly, there are no flights into Jackson from Seattle or Portland. If you're flying in from the Pacific Northwest, you will need to go through Salt Lake City, a 275-mile rental car drive from Jackson.

Airport Shuttles and Taxis

Alltrans/Gray Line of Jackson Hole (307/733-3135 or 800/443-6133, www.jacksonholealltrans.com) provides airport shuttle service to and from motels in Jackson ($16 one-way or $31 round-trip per person) and Teton Village ($26 one-way or $47 round-trip per person). The shuttles meet nearly all commercial airline flights in winter and most summertime flights, but you should make reservations to be sure of an airport pickup. Make outgoing reservations for a motel pickup 24 hours in advance.

From the airport, one-way taxi rates for one or two people are $32 to Jackson, or $55 to Teton Village. At last count there were 24(!) local taxi companies, including **Buckboard Transportation** (307/733-1112 or 877/791-0211, www.buckboardtrans.com), **Bullseye Taxi** (307/730-5000), **Cowboy Cab** (307/413-1000, www.cowboycab.net), **Old West Taxi** (307/690-8898), **Old Faithful Taxi** (307/699-4020, www.oldfaithfultaxi.com), **Teton Taxi** (307/733-1506), and **Westbank Cab** (307/690-0112).

BY BUS
Long-Distance Buses
Greyhound buses don't come even close to Jackson; the nearest stopping place is the regional hub at Salt Lake City. **Mountain States Express/Alltrans** (307/733-3135 or 800/652-9510, www.mountainstatesexpress.com) has year-round daily service connecting Jackson with Salt Lake City ($70 one-way) and Idaho Falls ($35 one-way) daily. Along the way, vans pass through Star Valley, Cokeville, Kemmerer, Evanston, Park City, Rexburg, Tetonia, Driggs, and Victor, and you can also get on or off at any of these towns.

Salt Lake Express (208/656-8824 or 800/356-9796, www.saltlakeexpress.com) runs shuttle vans connecting Jackson with Idaho Falls three times daily for $39 one-way. The company also has daily service south to Salt Lake ($67), north to West Yellowstone and Butte, and west to Twin Falls and Boise.

START Buses
Local buses are operated by Southern Teton Area Rapid Transit (START, 307/733-4521, www.startbus.com) and serve Jackson and Teton Village all year. START fares are **free** within town and $3 one-way to Teton Village ($1.50 for seniors and children). Discount coupons are available for multiple rides. Hours of operation are generally 6 A.M.–10:30 P.M. During summer and winter, buses run seven days a week, with in-town service every half-hour. Service to Teton Village is hourly (more or less) in summer and two or three times an hour in winter. Reduced bus service is available in fall and spring. Get schedules and route maps in the visitor center. Buses stop near most Jackson hotels and motels and are equipped to carry skis (in winter) and bikes (in summer) on outside racks. Unfortunately, START buses do not run to the airport, Kelly, or Moose, but commuter buses ($8 one-way) provide morning and evening service to Teton Valley, Idaho (Driggs and Victor), as well as Star Valley.

CAR AND RV RENTALS
Most of the national chains offer rental cars in town or at the airport. These include **Alamo** (307/733-0671 or 888/426-3299, www.alamo.com), **Avis** (307/733-3422 or 800/831-2847, www.avis.com), **Budget** (270 W. Pearl St., 307/733-2206 or 800/237-7251, www.budget.com), **Dollar** (345 W. Broadway Ave., 307/733-9224 or 877/222-7736, www.dollar.com), **Hertz** (307/733-2272 or 800/654-3131, www.hertz.com), **National** (220 N. Millward St., 307/733-7961 or 888/868-6204, www.nationalcar.com), and **Thrifty** (307/734-9306 or 800/847-4389, www.jackson.thrifty.com). Alamo, Avis, Hertz, and National all have counters at the airport, while the others provide a free shuttle to their in-town offices. **Leisure Sports** (1075 S. Hwy. 89, 307/733-3040, www.leisuresportsadventure.com) also has a few rental cars.

The best deals are often from Dollar or Thrifty, but check one of the online reservation sources (www.travelocity.com or www.expedia.com) to see who currently has the best rates. You may be better off getting a car in town, where you don't have to pay the additional taxes imposed at the airport. Taxes and fees (especially for airport rentals) can add another 21 percent to your charges, so read the fine print! Reserve cars at least one month ahead during summer and two months ahead for midsummer or the Christmas–New Year's holiday period. Be sure to mention any discounts; an AAA membership generally cuts 10 percent from the bill.

PARK TOURS

Summertime bus tours of Grand Teton and Yellowstone national parks are available several times a week from **Gray Line of Jackson Hole/Alltrans** (307/733-3135 or 800/443-6133, www.graylinejh.com). Yellowstone tours last 11 hours and cost $115, while eight-hour Grand Teton tours are $100; rates for kids are half-price. Add a $12 park entrance fee to both tours. During winter, Gray Line/Alltrans has daily bus runs to Flagg Ranch Resort for $106 round-trip, arriving in time to meet the snowcoach departures for Yellowstone. Reservations required. Jackson taxi companies also offer shuttle services within the park and guided tours.

Operated by Teton Science School, **Wildlife Expeditions** (307/733-2623 or 888/945-3567, www.wildlifeexpeditions.org) leads an array of wildlife-viewing safaris throughout the region, from four-hour sunset trips for $125 to four-day tours through Yellowstone and Grand Teton for $1,995. Their trips change seasonally—depending upon which animals are visible—and are offered in customized vehicles with multiple roof hatches for better wildlife viewing.

Get a geologist's perspective on the area from **Earth Tours** (307/733-4261, www.earth-tours.com), with outstanding tours and hikes led by Dr. Keith Watts. He also guides full-day trips into Yellowstone and longer trips to southern Utah parks.

Other companies with guided van tours of the area include **Ana's Grand Excursions** (307/690-6106, www.anasgrandexcursions.com), **Brushbuck Guide Services** (888/282-5868, www.brushbuckphototours.com), **Callowishus Park Touring Company** (307/413-5483, www.callowishus.com), **EcoTour Adventures** (307/690-9533, www.jhecotouradventures.com), **Upstream Anglers and Outdoor Adventures** (307/739-9443 or 800/642-8979, www.upstreamanglers.com), **Grand Teton Adventure Company** (307/734-4454 or 800/700-1558, www.grandtetonadventures.com), **The Hole Hiking Experience** (307/690-4453 or 866/733-4453, www.holehike.com), and **VIP Adventure Travel** (307/699-1077, www.vipadventuretravel.com).

Information and Services

INFORMATION

On the north side of town is the **Jackson Hole & Greater Yellowstone Visitor Center** (532 N. Cache Dr., 307/733-3316, www.jacksonholechamber.com, open daily). Brochures are also available at the airport, the stagecoach stop on Town Square, next to the downtown public restrooms at Cache and Gill, and at the Mangy Moose in Teton Village. Immediately south of the visitor center is an impressive building housing the **Wyoming Game and Fish** (307/733-2321) offices.

The **Bridger-Teton National Forest** supervisor's office (340 N. Cache Dr., 307/739-5500, www.fs.fed.us/r4/btnf) is open Monday–Friday 8 A.M.–4:30 P.M. Get information and Forest Service maps at the visitor center.

Kid-Friendly Jackson

During summer, older kids will enjoy hiking, mountain biking, Snake River float and whitewater trips, the shoot-out, and the putting course at Alpine Miniature Golf. In winter, snowboarding and skiing are favorites of older kids, but sleigh rides, dogsledding, ice-skating, and snowshoeing are also fun. While in town, be sure to pick up a copy of the free *Teton Family Magazine* (www.tetonfamily.wordpress.com), with articles on life beneath these majestic peaks.

For those traveling with tots, **Baby's Away** (307/739-4711 or 888/616-8495, www.babysaway.com) and **Babies on the Go** (307/690-6746, www.babiesonthego-jh.com) rent all sorts of baby supplies, including car seats, cribs, gates, joggers, backpacks, swings, and high chairs.

You'll find more stroller and backpack rentals—along with trendy kids' clothing—at **Teton Kids** (130 E. Broadway Ave., 307/739-2176). **Second Helpings** (141 E. Pearl Ave., 307/733-9466) has an excellent selection of quality used baby and children's clothes.

For child care, contact **Jackson Hole Babysitting** (307/732-7720, www.jacksonholebabysitting.com), **Playtime in the Tetons** (307/734-0153, www.playtimeinthetetons.com), or **Snake River Babysitting & Nannies** (307/699-1195, www.facebook.com).

Jackson Hole Mountain Resort (307/733-2292 or 888/333-7766, www.jacksonhole.com, Mon.–Sat. mid-June–early Sept. and daily late Nov.–early Apr.) operates a Kids Ranch day camp with activities and child care for ages 6 months–11 years old. Programs are geared to different ages and cost $89 per day.

Library

Spacious **Teton County Library** (125 Virginian La., 307/733-2164, www.tclib.org) is the kind of library every town should have. Inside this modern building is a large collection of books about Wyoming and the West, plus a great kids' section (complete with a fenced-in children's garden with a tepee). Computers provide free Internet access and are available by reservation or on a walk-up-and-wait basis. In the summer the queue can get long if you don't have a reservation. The library takes reservations up to one week in advance. Library hours are 10 A.M.–8 P.M. Monday–Thursday, 10 A.M.–5:30 P.M. Friday, and 1–5 P.M. Saturday–Sunday. If you plan to be in the Jackson area for a week or more, it may be worth your while to get a visitor's library card. For a one-time fee of $10 you can check out up to four books at a time. (Completion of a major library addition is expected in 2013.)

JACKSON HOLE FOR KIDS

Those traveling with children will find an abundance of kid-friendly options in Jackson Hole. A few noteworthy examples include:

- the hands-on **Children's Discovery Gallery** at the **National Museum of Wildlife Art**

- playgrounds at **Mike Yokel Jr. Park** (Kelly and Hall Streets), **Miller Park** (Powderhorn Lane and Maple Way), and **Baux Park** (base of Snow King Mountain)

- the excellent swimming pool and corkscrew water slide at the **Teton County Recreation Center**

- the fine children's section of the library

- chuck-wagon dinners at **Bar-T-Five** or **Bar J**

- pizzas at the **Calico** (where the lawn is great for kids)

- melodramas at **Jackson Hole Playhouse**

- the **Alpine Slide** at **Snow King Resort**

- the chairlifts, bungee trampoline, climbing wall, and pop-jet fountain at **Jackson Hole Resort**

- the evening shootouts at **Town Square**

- horseback or wagon rides

- float trips down the Snake River

- a trip to the fish hatchery

- a night at the rodeo (including the kids-only calf chase)

- the weird and wacky collection of oddities at **Ripley's Believe It or Not!**

- a boat ride and hike at **Jenny Lake** inside Grand Teton National Park

- day camp at the recreation center (grades 1-6)

Newspapers

Jackson's outstanding local newspaper—the *Jackson Hole News and Guide* (307/733-2047, www.jhnewsandguide.com)—is produced in tabloid format. Free Monday–Saturday editions can be found all over the valley, and a fat weekly edition ($0.50) comes out on Wednesdays with more detailed local and regional coverage, including the weekly entertainment paper, *Stepping Out*. The free *Jackson Hole Weekly* (307/732-0299, www.planetjh.com) focuses on local music, art, and entertainment, with a variety of topical stories about the region.

Radio

Find **National Public Radio's KUWJ** on your dial at 90.3 FM (www.wyomingpublicradio.net). The locals' commercial station is **KMTN** (www.kmtnthemountain.com) at 96.9 FM.

At 89.1 FM, radio station **KHOL** (www.jhcr.org) is a nonprofit community station with a wide variety of music—free from ads—hosted by local DJs. Other Jackson Hole radio stations are KZJH 95.3 FM and KSGT 1340 AM. See www.jacksonholeradio.com for details on the commercial stations.

Weddings

Jackson Hole makes a wonderful spot for a mountain wedding, with a grand setting, an abundance of fine lodging places and upscale caterers, plus easy access from anywhere in the nation. You can choose the simple back-to-nature version with a couple of family members along Jenny Lake or the full-blown variety at such places as Rancho Alegre Lodge (over $10,000 with the four-night minimum). A local company produces a slick 100-page free magazine called *A Grand Wedding* (www.jacksonholewedding.com), packed with advice and ads for Jackson Hole caterers, locations, musicians, DJs, photographers, wedding consultants, spas, tent and carriage rentals, wedding cakes, limos, and yes, even portable toilets. Pick up a copy at the visitor center or order one from their website.

Also check out **Destination Jackson Hole** (307/734-5007, www.destinationjacksonhole.com) for wedding planning.

Looking for a stunning natural setting to tie the knot? Book your wedding at **Chapel of the Transfiguration** (307/733-2603, www.stjohnsjackson.org) or **Chapel of the Sacred Heart** (307/733-2516, www.olmcatholic.org) within Grand Teton National Park, but be ready to drop $1,500 or so to reserve a date.

For specifics on obtaining marriage licenses, contact the Teton County Clerk (307/733-7733, www.tetonwyo.org).

SERVICES

Jackson's main **post office** (1070 Maple Way, 307/733-3650) near Powderhorn Lane is open 8:30 A.M.–5 P.M. Monday–Friday and 10 A.M.–1 P.M. Saturday. Other post offices are downtown (220 W. Pearl Ave., 307/739-1740), in Teton Village (307/733-3575), in Wilson (307/733-3335), and in Kelly (307/733-8884).

For shipping, packaging, and copying needs, head to the **UPS Store** (970 W. Broadway Ave., 307/733-9250, www.theupsstore.com).

Wash clothes at **Broadway Laundry** (860 W. Broadway Ave., 307/734-7627).

Showers ($6 with a towel) are available from **Anvil Motel** (215 N. Cache Dr., 307/733-3668 or 800/234-4507, www.anvilmotel.com).

Banking

Get fast cash from **ATMs** at many locations around town, including banks, grocers, downtown shops, the airport, plus in Teton Village and the Aspens.

International travelers will appreciate the currency exchange where you can swap those euros, Japanese yen, or colorful Canadian dollars at all four **Wells Fargo** (307/733-3737, www.wellsfargo.com) locations: 112 Center Street, 50 Buffalo Way, Teton Village, and in the Aspens on Teton Village Road.

Internet

To keep in touch with folks via email, use the

SAVING JACKSON HOLE

Over the last 30 years, Jackson has grown from a sleepy burg to a national focal point for outdoor fun. The population nearly doubled between 1990 and 2000. Growth has since slowed – especially with the recession that began in 2008 – but by 2010 almost 10,000 people lived in Jackson. Expensive homes have spread across old ranch lands, retailers such as Kmart moved in, and development now reaches for miles south from Jackson itself. Surrounding towns such as Alpine, Driggs, and Afton have become bedroom communities for those willing to endure the long commute to Jackson, and their growth spreads the problems outward.

Although 97 percent of the land in Teton County is in the public domain, the 70,000 acres of private land that remain are rapidly being developed, and Jackson Hole is in grave danger of losing the wild beauty that has attracted visitors for more than a century. This dilemma is immediately obvious to anyone arriving in Jackson. The edges of town have fallen under a proliferation of trophy homes, real-estate offices, chain motels, fast-food outlets, mega-marts, gas stations, and elaborate banks, all competing beneath a thicket of signs. Summertime traffic jams are becoming all too common in this once-quiet place, where more than 35,000 visitors can be found on a summer afternoon.

Way back in 1994, Jackson voters got fed up with the pace of development and voted to scrap the town's 2 percent lodging tax, which had provided more than $1 million per year in funding to promote Jackson Hole around the world. Despite this lack of promotional effort, growth has continued. A moratorium on large commercial developments went into effect in 2008, but smaller developments with housing for employees were allowed.

The **Jackson Hole Conservation Alliance** (307/733-9417, www.jhalliance.com) is a 1,800-member environmental group that works to preserve the remaining natural areas of Jackson Hole. Membership starts at $30 per year and includes biannual newsletters and a chance to help control the many developments that threaten this still-beautiful valley.

Another influential local group is the **Jackson Hole Land Trust** (307/733-4707, www.jhlandtrust.org). Established in 1980, this nonprofit organization obtains conservation easements to maintain ranches and other land threatened by development. The group has protected more than 20,000 acres in the valley in this way, including the 1,740-acre Walton Ranch, visible along the highway between Jackson and Wilson.

free terminals in the **public library.** Many local restaurants and coffee shops—even the Albertson's grocery store—provide free Wi-Fi.

Check out the current conditions around Jackson at the following **Web camera** sites: www.wyoroad.info and www.alltravelcams.com; the latter includes cameras in Town Square, the airport, Spring Creek Ranch, and Teton Valley, plus other regional webcams.

A great place to begin your Web tour is the chamber of commerce site: www.jacksonholechamber.com. Also very useful are www.jacksonholetraveler.com and www.jacksonholenet.com. All three of these contain links to dozens of local businesses of all types. You may also want to check out the Teton County website, www.tetonwyo.org. Federal government websites for the local area include Grand Teton National Park at www.nps.gov/grte, Yellowstone National Park at www.nps.gov/yell, Bridger-Teton National Forest at www.fs.fed.us/r4/btnf, and Caribou-Targhee National Forest at www.fs.fed.us/r4/caribou-targhee.

Medical

Because of the abundance of ski and snowboard accidents, orthopedic specialists are in high demand in Jackson and are some of the best around. The experts at **Teton Orthopaedics** (555 E. Broadway Ave., 307/733-3900 or 800/659-1335, www.tetonortho.com) are official physicians for the U.S. national ski team! **St. John's Medical Center** (625 E. Broadway Ave., 307/733-3636, www.tetonhospital.org) has emergency medical services. They also operate a winter-only ski-in (hobble in?) clinic at Teton Village (307/739-2650), along with a walk-in clinic next to the Smith's store, **Urgent Care of Jackson Hole** (1415 S. Hwy. 89, 307/739-8999). Another option is **Emerg-A-Care** (982 W. Broadway Ave., 307/733-8002) in the Powderhorn Mall.

Pets

Several local kennels in Jackson will keep an eye on Fido for you. **Happy Tails Pet Resort/ Spring Creek Animal Hospital** (1035 W. Broadway Ave., 307/733-1606, www.springcreekanimalhospital.com) provides veterinary care and kennels. **Rally's Pet Garage** (520 S. Hwy. 89, 307/733-7704, www.rallyspetgarage.com) is a unique service with "doggie daycare," boarding, dog baths, and grooming.

Photography

D. D. Camera Corral (60 S. Cache, 307/733-3831) is the local photo shop, with a good selection of professional and point-and-shoot equipment.

Serious professional or semipro photographers should not miss **Photography at the Summit** (303/295-7770 or 800/745-3211, www.photographyatthesummit.com), an extraordinary five-day series of workshops led by internationally famous photographers and photo editors. The staff always includes a contingent of *National Geographic* photographers.

Evening talks—held at the National Museum of Wildlife Art—are open to the public. Also notable are photography workshops through **Jackson Hole Center for the Arts** (240 S. Glenwood, 307/734-8956, www.jhcenterforthearts.org).

Recycling

Jackson has been at the forefront of the movement to practice the three R's: reduce, reuse, and recycle. Many businesses have attempted to go green (or at least to gain good publicity by saying all the right things). Even the ski resorts have gotten in on the action. Jackson Hole Mountain Resort—one of the largest users of energy in the valley—is committed to getting 50 percent of its energy from renewables such as wind, biomass, small hydro, and geothermal. **Reduce, Reuse, Recycle Jackson Hole** (www.howdoyourrr.com) recognizes local businesses that promote conservation.

Just because you're on vacation doesn't mean you should just chuck everything in the trash. If you don't need that extra plastic bag or napkin, don't take it. Bring your coffee mug instead of getting a throwaway cup. Walk or bike instead of driving around town. Even the small steps add up.

Jackson has a good recycling program and accepts newspaper, aluminum cans, glass, tin cans, plastic milk jugs, magazines, catalogs, cardboard, and office paper. The **recycling center** (307/733-7678, www.tetonwyo.org/recycling) is the big brown building two miles south of the high school on U.S. Highway 89, but bins are also located on the rodeo grounds on the corner of Snow King Avenue and Flat Creek Drive, the recreation center on East Gill, and in Teton Village.

Bridger-Teton National Forest

One of the largest national forests in the Lower 48, Bridger-Teton ("the B-T") National Forest stretches southward for 135 miles from the Yellowstone border and covers 3.4 million acres. In Jackson Hole, the two areas of most interest for recreation are the Teton Wilderness and the Gros Ventre Wilderness, but nonwilderness areas offer additional opportunities for recreation.

The Bridger-Teton National Forest **supervisor's office** (307/739-5500, www. fs.fed.us/r4/btnf) is at 340 North Cache Drive in Jackson. The **Jackson Hole & Greater Yellowstone Visitor Center** (532 N. Cache Dr., 307/733-3316, www.jacksonholechamber. com, open daily), a couple of blocks north on Cache, has a Forest Service worker on duty who can provide recreation information. The center usually sells Bridger-Teton maps and has a good choice of outdoor books. Local ranger stations are the **Jackson Ranger District** (directly behind the supervisor's office, 307/739-5400) and the **Buffalo Ranger District** (nine miles east of Moran Junction, 307/543-2386).

TETON WILDERNESS

The Teton Wilderness covers 585,468 acres of mountain country, bordered to the north by Yellowstone National Park, to the west by Grand Teton National Park, and to the east by the Washakie Wilderness. Established as a primitive area in 1934, it was declared one of the nation's first wilderness areas upon passage of the 1964 Wilderness Act. The Teton Wilderness offers a diverse mixture of rolling lands carpeted with lodgepole pine, spacious grassy meadows, roaring rivers, and dramatic mountains. Elevations range from 7,500 feet to the 12,165-foot summit of Younts Peak. The Continental Divide slices across the wilderness, with headwaters of the Yellowstone River draining the eastern half and headwaters of the Buffalo and Snake Rivers flowing down the western side. Teton Wilderness has a considerable amount of bear activity, so make sure you

know how to avoid bear encounters and bring pepper spray.

One of the most unusual places within Teton Wilderness is **Two Ocean Creek,** where a creek abruptly splits at a rock and the two branches never rejoin. One branch becomes Atlantic Creek, and its waters eventually reach the Atlantic Ocean, while the other becomes Pacific Creek and its waters flow to the Snake River, the Columbia River, and thence into the Pacific Ocean! Mountain man Osborne Russell described this phenomenon in 1835:

On the South side about midway of the prairie stands a high snowy peak from whence issues a Stream of water which after entering the plain it divides equally one half running West and other East thus bidding adieu to each other one bound for the Pacific and the other for the Atlantic ocean. Here a trout of 12 inches in length may cross the mountains in safety. Poets have sung of the "meeting of the waters" and fish climbing cataracts but the "parting of the waters and fish crossing mountains" I believe remains unsung yet by all except the solitary Trapper who sits under the shade of a spreading pine whistling blankverse and beating time to the tune with a whip on his trap sack whilst musing on the parting advice of these waters.

Natural events have had a major effect on the Teton Wilderness. On July 21, 1987, a world-record high-elevation tornado created a 10,000-acre blowdown of trees around the Enos Lake area, and it took years to rebuild the trails. A series of fires followed—including the Huck and Mink Creek fires that burned 200,000 acres. Don't let these incidents dissuade you from visiting; this is still a marvelous and little-used area, and more than 60 percent of the land was not burned. Herds of elk graze in alpine areas, and many consider the Thorofare country abutting Yellowstone

National Park the most remote place in the Lower 48. This is prime grizzly habitat and you may well encounter them, so be very cautious at all times. Poles for hanging food have been placed at most campsites, as have bear-resistant boxes or barrels. Use them, and always keep a clean camp. You can rent bear-resistant backpacker food tubes or horse panniers from the Buffalo Ranger District (307/543-2386), but it's a good idea to make reservations for these items before your trip.

Access

Three primary trailheads provide access to the Teton Wilderness: Pacific Creek on the southwestern end, Turpin Meadow on the Buffalo Fork River, and Brooks Lake just east of the Continental Divide. Campgrounds are at each of these trailheads. Teton Wilderness is a favorite of Wyomingites, particularly those with horses, and in the fall elk hunters from across the nation come here. Distances are so great and some of the stream crossings so intimidating that few backpackers head into this wilderness area. No permits are needed, but it's a good idea to stop in at the **Buffalo Ranger District** (307/543-2386), nine miles east of Moran Junction on U.S. Highway 26/287, for topographic maps and information on current trail conditions, bear problems, regulations, and a list of permitted outfitters offering horse or llama trips.

For a shorter trip, you could take a guided horseback ride at the Turpin Meadow Trailhead with **Yellowstone Outfitters** (307/543-2418 or 800/447-4711, www.yellowstoneoutfitters.com) or **Buffalo Valley Ranch** (307/543-2062 or 888/543-2477, www.buffalovalleyranch.com). **Teton Horseback Adventures** (307/730-8829, www.horsebackadv.com) heads out from the Pacific Creek Trailhead. All three of these outfitters offer pack trips into the Teton Wilderness.

Unfortunately, USGS maps don't show the many Teton Wilderness trails built and maintained (or not maintained) by private outfitters and hunters. These can make hiking confusing, since not every junction is signed. Forest Service maps for the wilderness have been updated with most trail locations. A few of the many possible hikes are described as follows.

Whetstone Creek

Whetstone Creek Trail begins at the Pacific Creek Trailhead, on the southwest side of Teton Wilderness. An enjoyable 20-mile round-trip hike leaves the trailhead and follows Pacific Creek for 1.5 miles before splitting left to follow Whetstone Creek. Bear left when the trail splits again another three miles upstream and continue through a series of small meadows to the junction with Pilgrim Creek Trail. Turn right here and follow this trail two more miles to Coulter Creek Trail, climbing up Coulter Creek to scenic Coulter Basin and then dropping along the East Fork of Whetstone Creek. This rejoins the Whetstone Creek Trail and returns you to the trailhead, passing many attractive small meadows along the way. The upper half of this loop hike was burned in 1988; some areas were heavily scorched, while others are patchy. Flowers are abundant in the burned areas, and this is important elk habitat.

South Fork to Soda Fork

A fine loop hike leaves Turpin Meadow and follows South Buffalo Fork River to South Fork Falls. Just above this point, a trail splits off and climbs to Nowlin Meadow (excellent views of Smokehouse Mountain) and then down to Soda Fork River, where it joins the Soda Fork Trail. Follow this trail back downstream to huge Soda Fork Meadow (a good place to see moose and occasionally grizzlies) and then back to Turpin Meadow, a distance of approximately 23 miles round-trip. For a fascinating side trip from this route, head up the Soda Fork into the alpine at Crater Lake, a six-mile hike above the Nowlin Meadow–Soda Fork Trail junction. The outlet stream at Crater Lake disappears into a gaping hole, emerging as a large creek two miles below at Big Springs. It's an incredible sight.

Cub Creek Area

The Brooks Lake area just east of Togwotee Pass is a popular summertime camping and fishing place with magnificent views. Brooks Lake Trail follows the western shore of Brooks Lake and continues past Upper Brooks Lakes to Bear Cub Pass. From here, the trail drops to Cub Creek, where you'll find several good campsites. You can make a long and scenic loop by following the trail up Cub Creek into the alpine country and then back down along the South Buffalo Fork River to Lower Pendergraft Meadow. From here, take the Cub Creek Trail back up along Cub Creek to Bear Cub Pass and back out to Brooks Lake. Get a topographic map before heading into this remote country. Total distance is approximately 33 miles round-trip.

GROS VENTRE WILDERNESS

The 287,000-acre Gros Ventre Wilderness was established in 1984 and covers the mountain country just east of Jackson Hole. This range trends mainly in a northwest-southeast direction and is probably best known for Sleeping Indian Mountain (maps now call it Sheep Mountain, but locals never use that appellation), the distinctive rocky summit visible from Jackson Hole. Although there are densely forested areas at lower elevations, the central section of the wilderness lies above timberline, and many peaks top 10,000 feet. The tallest is Doubletop Peak at 11,682 feet. The Tetons are visible from almost any high point in the Gros Ventre, and meadows line the lower-elevation streams. Elk, mule deer, bighorn sheep, moose, and black bears are found here, and a few grizzlies have been reported. The Forest Service office in Jackson has more information on the wilderness, including brief trail descriptions and maps.

Access and Trails

Several roads provide good access to the Gros Ventre Wilderness: Gros Ventre River Road on the northern border; Curtis Canyon Road on the western margin; and Granite Creek Road to the south. Flat Creek is rough and accessible only in a 4WD vehicle. Hikes beginning or ending in the Granite Creek area have the added advantage of nearby Granite Hot Springs, a great place to soak tired muscles.

For a beautiful hike, follow **Highline Trail** from the Granite Creek area across to Cache Creek, a distance of 16 miles. This route passes just below a row of high and rugged mountains, but because it isn't a loop route, you'll need to hitchhike or set up a shuttle back. Plan on three days for this hike. The area is crisscrossed with game and cattle trails, making it easy to get lost, especially on the headwaters of Little Granite Creek. Talk with Forest Service folks before heading out, and make sure that you know how to read a map and compass.

A third hike begins at the **Goosewing Ranger Station,** 12 miles east of Slide Lake on Gros Ventre River Road. Take the trail from here to Two Echo Park (a fine camping spot) and then continue up to Six Lakes. You can return via the same trail or take the Crystal Creek Trail back to Red Rock Ranch and hitch back to Goosewing. The trail distance is approximately 23 miles round-trip.

GRANITE HOT SPRINGS

At the head of a gorgeous mountain valley, Granite Hot Springs (307/734-7400, http://granitehotsprings.mountainmancountry.com) is a wonderful escape both summer and winter. Get here by driving south from Jackson 12 miles to Hoback Junction and then another 12 miles east on U.S. Highway 189 to the turnoff at Granite Creek Road. This well-maintained gravel road follows Granite Creek for 10 miles, affording impressive views of the Gros Ventre Range and the 50-foot drop of **Granite Falls.** The road ends at a parking lot just a short walk from the hot springs. The deep pool was built in 1933 by the Civilian Conservation Corps and recently improved with a deck and changing rooms. The pool stays around 93°F in the summer but rises to 112°F in winter when the water flow slows. The springs are open daily (10 A.M.–8 P.M. June–Oct., 10 A.M.–5 P.M. Dec.–Mar., $6 adults, $4 ages 3–12, and free for infants), but are closed in the fall and

© DON PITCHER

Granite Hot Springs

spring. No showers or running water are available at the pool, but vault toilets are nearby. Suits and towels can be rented, and a few snacks are sold here. Granite Canyon Road is not plowed in winter but is groomed for use by both snowmobilers and cross-country skiers. A nearby campground (mid-May–Sept., $15, no reservations) is managed by folks from the hot springs and almost never fills up. Dispersed camping is allowed on the road to Granite Hot Springs, except along the final 1.3 miles before the springs.

Caribou-Targhee National Forest

Covering nearly three million acres, Caribou-Targhee National Forest extends from Montana to Utah. Most of the forest lies within Idaho, but it also includes the western edge of Wyoming along the Tetons. Much of the forest is heavily logged, but two wilderness areas protect most of the Wyoming section. Contact the Forest Service office in Driggs, Idaho (208/354-2312, www.fs.fed.us/r4/caribou-targhee) for more recreation information.

Hiking

Many short hiking options are available on the west side of the Tetons, and the Forest Service office in Driggs has a handout that describes more than 20 of these hikes. A few of the best include the following. From Darby Canyon Trailhead, you can choose either the **Aspen Trail** (3.6 miles one-way; especially pretty in the fall) or the **South Darby Trail** (2.7 miles one-way; with nice waterfalls and flowered meadows). The latter leads to two remarkable caves that extend deep into the mountains: **Wind Cave** and **Ice Cave.** Hikers with flashlights can go a short distance into these caves, but very experienced spelunkers (with proper gear) have discovered miles of passageways connecting the two.

From the South Teton Trailhead, you can opt to climb **Table Mountain** (6.4 miles one-way), visit gorgeous **Alaska Basin** (7.7 miles one-way), or ascend the **Devil's Stairs** to Teton Shelf (6.8 miles one-way). All three of these hikes take you high into the alpine, but many families just hike until the kids get tired, eat lunch, and then head back to the car.

Several trails take off from the Teton Pass area along Wyoming Highway 22/Idaho Highway 33, including **Moose Creek Trail,** which leads to Moose Meadows (5.4 miles one-way), and the **Teton Crest Trail** if you're feeling very ambitious (nine miles one-way). It joins another popular hiking route, the **Coal Creek Trail,** for an alternative return route to the highway.

JEDEDIAH SMITH WILDERNESS

The 123,451-acre Jedediah Smith Wilderness lies on the west side of the Teton Range, facing Idaho but lying entirely within Wyoming. Access is primarily from the Idaho side, although trails breach the mountain passes at various points, making it possible to enter from Grand Teton National Park. This area was not declared a wilderness until 1984. A second wilderness area, the 10,820-acre **Winegar Hole Wilderness** (pronounced WINE-a-gur), lies along the southern border of Yellowstone National Park. Grizzlies love this country, but hikers will find it uninteresting and without trails. In contrast, the Jedediah Smith Wilderness contains nearly 200 miles of paths and some incredible high-mountain scenery.

Several mostly gravel roads lead up from the Driggs and Victor areas into the Tetons. Get a map showing wilderness trails and access points from the Caribou-Targhee National Forest ranger station in Driggs, Idaho (208/354-2312) or from the Forest Service offices in Jackson. Be sure to camp at least 200 feet from lakes and 100 feet from streams. Group size limits are also in place; check with the Forest Service for specifics on these and other backcountry regulations. In addition, anyone planning to cross into Grand Teton National Park from the west side will need to get a park camping permit in advance. Wilderness permits are not required for the Jedediah Smith Wilderness. Both grizzly and black bears are present throughout the Tetons, so all food must be either hung out of reach or stored in bear-resistant containers.

Hidden Corral Basin

At the northern end of the wilderness, Hidden Corral Basin provides a fine loop hike. Locals (primarily those on horseback) crowd this area on late-summer weekends. Get to the trailhead by driving north from Tetonia on Idaho Highway 32 to Lamont, then turn north on a gravel road. Follow it one mile and then turn right (east) onto Coyote Meadows Road. The trailhead is approximately 10 miles up, where the road dead-ends. An eight-mile trail parallels South Bitch Creek (the name Bitch Creek comes from the French word for a female deer, *biche*) to Hidden Corral, where you may see moose. Be sure to bring a fishing pole to try for the cutthroats.

Above Hidden Corral you can make a pleasant loop back by turning north onto the trail to Nord Pass and then dropping along the Carrot Ridge and Conant Basin Trails to Bitch Creek Trail and then on to Coyote Meadows, a distance of 21 miles round-trip. Note that this is grizzly and black bear country, and bear-resistant containers are required. By the way, Hidden Corral received its name in the outlaw days, when rustlers would steal horses in Idaho, change the brands, and hold the horses in this natural corral until the branding wounds healed. The horses were then sold to Wyoming ranchers. Owen Wister's *The Virginian* describes a pursuit of horse thieves through Bitch Creek country.

🄲 Alaska Basin

The most popular hiking trail in the Jedediah Smith Wilderness begins near the **Teton Canyon Campground** (518/885-3639 or 877/444-6777 for reservations, www.reservations.gov, open late May–mid-Sept., $10) and leads through flower-bedecked meadows to mountain-rimmed Alaska Basin. It's great country, but don't expect a true wilderness experience, because many others will also be hiking and camping here. Get to the campground by following the Grand Targhee Ski Resort signs east from Driggs, Idaho. A gravel road splits off to the right approximately three miles beyond the little settlement of Alta. Follow it to the campground. (If you miss the turn, you'll end up at the ski area.) For an enjoyable loop, follow Alaska Basin Trail up the canyon to Basin Lakes and then head southwest along the Teton Crest Trail to the Teton Shelf Trail. Follow this trail back to its junction with the Alaska Basin Trail, dropping down the Devil's Stairs—a series of very steep switchbacks. You can then take the Alaska Basin Trail back to Teton Campground, a round-trip distance of approximately 19 miles. You could also use these trails to reach the high peaks of the Tetons or to cross the mountains into Death Canyon within Grand Teton National Park (camping permit required). Campfires and horse camping are not allowed in Alaska Basin.

Moose Meadows

For a somewhat less crowded hiking experience, check out the Moose Meadows area on the southern end of the Jedediah Smith Wilderness. Get to the trailhead by going three miles southeast of Victor on Idaho Highway 33. Turn north (left) on Moose Creek Road and follow it to the trailhead. The trail parallels Moose Creek to Moose Meadows, a good place to camp. You'll need to ford the creek twice, so this trail is best hiked in late summer. At the meadows, the trail dead-ends into Teton Crest Trail, providing access to Grand Teton National Park through some gorgeous alpine country. A nice loop can be made by heading south along this trail to flower-covered Coal Creek Meadows. A trail leads from here past 10,068-foot Taylor Mountain (an easy side trip with magnificent views), down to Taylor Basin, through lodgepole forests, and then back to your starting point. This loop hike will take you 15 miles round-trip.

Teton Valley, Idaho

The west side of the Tetons differs dramatically from nearby Jackson Hole. As the road descends from Teton Pass into Teton Valley, Idaho (a.k.a. Pierre's Hole), the lush farming country spreads out before you, 30 miles long and 15 miles across. This, the "quiet side" of the Tetons, offers a slower pace than bustling Jackson, but the Teton Range vistas are equally dramatic.

In recent years the growth in Jackson Hole has spilled across the mountains. The potato farms, horse pastures, and country towns are now undergoing the same transformation that first hit Jackson in the 1970s. As land prices soar and affordable housing becomes more difficult to find in Jackson, more people have opted to move over the pass and commute from Idaho. Glossy ads now fill *Teton Valley Magazine,* offering ranchland with a view, luxurious log homes, cozy second homes, private aircraft hangars, espresso coffee, mountain-bike rentals, and handmade lodgepole furniture. Despite these changes, Teton Valley remains a laid-back place, and spud farming is still a part of the local economy. The primary town here—it's the county seat—is Driggs, with Victor nine miles south and tiny Tetonia eight miles north.

History

The area now known as Teton Valley was used for centuries by various Indian tribes, including the Bannock, Blackfeet, Crow, Gros Ventre, Shoshone, and Nez Perce. John Colter—a member of the Lewis and Clark expedition—was the first white man to reach this area, wandering through in the winter of 1807–1808. In 1931, an Idaho farmer claimed to have plowed up a stone carved into the shape of a human face, with "John Colter 1808" etched into the

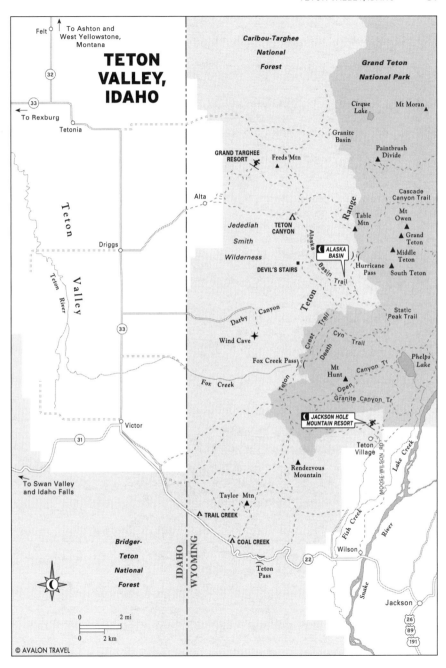

Felt
To Ashton and
West Yellowstone,
Montana

TETON VALLEY, IDAHO

32

33
To Rexburg

Tetonia

Caribou-Targhee
National
Forest

Grand Teton
National Park

Cirque
Lake

Mt Moran

Granite
Basin

Paintbrush
Divide

GRAND TARGHEE
RESORT

Freds Mtn

Alta

Cascade
Canyon Trail

Teton
Valley

Jedediah

Smith

Wilderness

Teton Range

TETON
CANYON

Table
Mtn

Mt
Owen

Grand
Teton

Middle
Teton

Alaska Basin

ALASKA
BASIN

Hurricane
Pass

South Teton

DEVIL'S STAIRS

Teton River

Darby   Canyon

Wind Cave

Teton Crest Trail

Static
Peak Trail

Cyn   Trail

Phelps
Lake

Death

Fox Creek Pass

Fox   Creek

Mt
Hunt

Canyon Tr

Open

Granite Canyon Tr

Victor

33

JACKSON HOLE
MOUNTAIN RESORT

Teton
Village

MOOSE-WILSON RD

Lake Creek

31

To Swan Valley
and Idaho Falls

Rendezvous
Mountain

Taylor Mtn

TRAIL CREEK

COAL CREEK

Teton
Pass

Fish Creek

Snake   River

Wilson

22

Jackson

26
89
191

Bridger-
Teton
National
Forest

IDAHO
WYOMING

0   2 mi

0   2 km

© AVALON TRAVEL

sides. The rock later turned out to be a hoax created by a man anxious to obtain a horse concession with Grand Teton National Park. He got the concession after donating the rock to the park museum.

Vieux Pierre, an Iroquois fur trapper for the Hudson's Bay Company, made this area his base in the 1820s, but was later killed by Blackfeet Indians in Montana. Many people still call the valley Pierre's Hole. Two fur trapper rendezvous took place in Pierre's Hole, but the 1832 event proved pivotal. About 1,000 Indians, trappers, and traders gathered for an annual orgy of trading, imbibing, and general partying. When a column of men on horseback appeared, two white trappers headed out for a meeting. The column turned out to be a group of Gros Ventre Indians, and the meeting quickly turned sour. One trapper shot the Gros Ventre chief point-blank, killing him. A battle quickly ensued that left 38 people dead on both sides and forced rendezvous participants to scatter. Later rendezvous were held in valleys where the animosities were not as high. For the next 50 years, virtually the only whites in Pierre's Hole were horse thieves and outlaws. Hiram C. Lapham was the first to try his hand at ranching in the valley, but his cattle were rustled by three outlaws, including Ed Harrington, alias Ed Trafton.

In 1888, a lawyer from Salt Lake City, B. W. Driggs, came to the valley and liked what he found. With his encouragement, a flood of Mormon settlers arrived in the next few years, establishing farms along the entire length of Teton Valley. By the 1940s the valley was home to a cheese factory, sawmills, a railroad line, and numerous sprawling ranches. Teton Valley's population plummeted in the 1960s, but in 1969 development began at Grand Targhee Ski Resort, and the economy started to turn around. Recent years have seen the area come into its own as tourism-related businesses began to eclipse farming and ranching. Over the last decade or so the valley has boomed, making Teton County, Idaho one of the fastest-growing counties (on a percentage basis) in the nation.

Teton Valley Recreation

Outdoor enthusiasts will discover all sorts of activities at all times of the year in the Driggs

Teton Range, as seen from Teton Valley

© DON PITCHER

area. The Teton River runs the entire length of Teton Valley and is renowned among fly-fishing enthusiasts, canoeists, and bird-watchers. A plethora of hikes can be found both to the east in the Tetons and to the west in the Big Hole Mountains. The Forest Service office in Driggs has details on other hiking options if you're looking for a less crowded experience.

The nonprofit **Friends of the Teton River** (36 E. Little Ave., 208/354-3871, www.tetonwater.org) works to preserve the Teton Basin.

The **National Outdoor Leadership School** (NOLS, 166 E. 200 S., 208/354-8443, www.nols.edu) has an office off the main road south of Driggs; headquarters is in Lander, Wyoming. The Driggs office—housed in an old Mormon church—runs summertime backpacking and whitewater training, plus backcountry skiing classes in the winter. Courses last 2–3 weeks.

Kids and their parents will appreciate the **Driggs Town Park,** with an attractive playground and sprinklers that make for impromptu summer fun. It's on Ashley Street. A paved **bike path** parallels Highway 33 between Victor and Driggs, providing a pleasant running, cycling, or inline skating opportunity. A wide bike lane heads east from Driggs all the way to the Targhee Resort. The nonprofit **Teton Valley Trails & Pathways** (208/201-1622, www.tvtap.org) has online maps showing local routes.

Peaked Sports (70 E. Little Ave., 208/354-2354 or 800/705-2354, www.peakedsports.com) rents mountain bikes, bike trailers, and kayaks in the summer, along with skis, snowboards, and snowshoes in the winter. Stop by for a helpful biking map ($12) of the area.

High Peaks Health and Fitness Center (50 Ski Hill Rd., 208/354-3128, www.highpeakspt.com) has $10 day passes.

The Links at Teton Peaks (127 N. 400 W., 208/456-2374) is a Scottish-style nine-hole golf course.

Horseback rides and pack trips are available from **Dry Ridge Outfitters** (208/354-2284, www.dryridge.com) or nearby Grand Targhee Ski Resort (in Alta, 307/353-2300 or 800/827-4433, www.grandtarghee.com). For horseback rides and winter sleigh rides, head to **Linn Canyon Ranch** (130 E. 600 S., 208/787-5466, www.linncanyonranch.com).

Bagley's Teton Mountain Ranch (265 W. 800 S., 208/787-9005 or 866/787-9005, www.elkadventures.com) raises more than 100 elk as breeding stock and for their antlers. It offers summertime wagon rides and wintertime sleigh rides among the elk for $9, plus horseback rides (starting at $35 for a one-hour ride).

Teton Aviation Center (208/354-3100 or 800/472-6382, www.tetonaviation.com) is best known for its scenic glider flights ($250 for a one-hour flight) past the Tetons, but it also offers airplane rides and has an impressive collection of vintage military aircraft.

Teton Balloon Flights (208/787-5500 or 866/533-6404, www.tetonballooning.com) offers one-hour hot-air balloon flights over Teton Valley for $265 per person in the summer.

Teton Valley Events

The main summer event, the **Teton Valley Summer Festival** (208/354-2500), comes on Fourth of July weekend. Highlights include hot-air balloon launches (more than 40 balloons) and tethered rides for the kids at the airport, a parade and crafts fair in Victor, a rodeo in Tetonia, arts exhibits, a pig roast, live music, and evening fireworks in Driggs.

Grand Targhee Ski Resort pulls out the stops for the always-popular **Targhee Bluegrass Festival** (307/353-2300 or 800/827-4433, www.grandtarghee.com) in mid-August, with nationally known acts. The music attracts a throng, so make camping or lodging reservations well ahead of time.

In mid-August, the **Teton County Fair** (208/354-2961) brings down-home fun with livestock judging, arts and crafts, quilts, and pies, jams, and other fare on display.

On Thursday evenings in July and August, **Music on Main** (208/201-5356, www.tetonvalleyfoundation.org) brings free concerts (two bands nightly) to Victor City Park. This is a surprisingly big deal, attracting nationally known acts.

VICTOR

Twenty-four miles west of Jackson, the town of Victor, Idaho, was—until recently—little more than the proverbial wide spot in the road. But things have changed dramatically as the population doubled in just five years and an ugly sprawl of homes and businesses covered former ranchland. Despite this, the town does have a couple of places worth noting.

Accommodations

Trails End Motel (208/787-2973, $80 d) rents simple four-person log cabin units with microwaves and fridges and is open May–mid-October.

Two miles south of town on Pole Canyon Road, **Kasper's Kountryside Inn** (208/787-2726, www.kasperskountrysideinn.com, $89–109 for up to four) is a barnlike building with two modern apartments with full kitchens.

Teton Springs is more evidence of the spillover effect from Jackson. This private club for the moneyed class includes 500 homes and condos, a golf course, a spa, tennis courts, a swimming pool, and an "old town village" with shopping, dining, lodging, and more. A heliport waits for those who can afford the helicopter flight over to Jackson for the evening. Various lodging options are offered at **Teton Springs Lodge & Spa** (208/787-7888 or 877/787-8757, www.tetonspringslodge.com), including luxurious hotel rooms ($237 d) and suites ($336–504 d). Condos and sprawling four-bedroom "cabins" are also available on a nightly or weekly basis.

On the north end of town, **Cowboy Roadhouse Lodge** (381 N. Agate St., 208/787-2755, www.cowboyroadhouselodge.com, $119 d) is a modern two-story motel with log beds, Wi-Fi, and two queen or one king bed.

Set on four acres and surrounded by cottonwood trees, **Fox Creek Inn Bed and Breakfast** (27 E. 550 South, 208/787-3333, www.thefoxcreekinn.com) has three guest rooms with queen beds and private baths ($139 d), plus a more spacious room with king bed, private bath, and indoor Jacuzzi ($185 d). All include a full breakfast, access to the outdoor hot tub,

and Wi-Fi. Fox Creek is halfway between Victor and Driggs.

Camping

The Forest Service's pleasant **Trail Creek Campground** (518/885-3639 or 877/444-6777, www.recreation.gov, open mid-May–mid-Sept., $10) is six miles southeast of Victor and just across the Wyoming state line. **Teton Valley Campground** (208/787-2647 or 877/787-3036, www.tetonvalleycampground.com), one mile west of Victor on Idaho Highway 31, has RV hookups ($28–41), tent sites ($22), basic cabins ($45), plus a small heated outdoor pool, a playground, and Wi-Fi.

Food

Victor Emporium (208/787-2221, www.victoremporium.com, daily 8 A.M.–6 P.M.) houses an old-fashioned soda fountain with huckleberry shakes in season, plus sundaes, banana splits, and cones year-round. It's been in business since 1949, and also sells fishing supplies and Idaho souvenirs.

Housed in an old one-car garage, **Grumpy's Goat Shack** (37 S. Main St., 208/787-2092, www.goatshack.com, daily 11 A.M.–9 P.M. Apr.–Oct., till 11 P.M. summer weekends) is a fun hot-dog stand/wine bar where Mike and Liz serve the best brats you'll ever taste, along with hot Italian beef sandwiches, chili-cheese dogs, charbroiled burgers, and Chicago-style hot dogs. They're the real deal; even true Chicagoans love 'em. The owners' goat produces milk for homemade goat cheese, served with roasted garlic and bread. The ceiling is crowded with bras and panties left by previous female customers (free drinks are the incitement). Sit outside around the patio tables. Credit cards are not accepted, but everything's under $9.

A cozy little brunch nook, **Sun Dog Café** (208/787-3354, daily 7 A.M.–3 P.M., $6–10) has a full espresso bar, with delicious pastries and local chocolates filling the display case. Eggs Benedict or French toast with bacon are good breakfast choices. For lunch, try a mahimahi taco or grilled steak salad.

Also in Victor is **Knotty Pine Supper Club** (208/787-2866, www.knottypinesupperclub.com, 11 A.M.–10 P.M., bar open until 1 A.M.), with hearty ribs, steaks, and rack of lamb. Most entrées are $10–25, but you can always choose the $10 dinner of hot turkey, meatloaf, mashed potatoes, and gravy. Knotty Pine is an old-fashioned place with low ceilings, log walls, and a dark interior brightened by blue Christmas lights. Dining is also available on the outside deck. Live bands crank out the dance tunes most nights and the bar is entirely smoke-free.

Amazingly, there are two microbreweries in Victor. In existence since 1988, **Grand Teton Brewing Company** (208/787-9000, www.grandtetonbrewing.com, 1–8 P.M. Mon.–Fri., 2–7 P.M. Sat.–Sun.) is on the east end of town. Drop by to sample Teton Ale, Old Faithful Ale, Bitch Creek ESB, Howling Wolf Weisse Bier, or Sweetgrass IPA. The gift shop (9 A.M.–5 P.M. Mon.–Fri.) sells T-shirts, glasses, and beer to go.

Much smaller is **Wildlife Brewing and Pizza** (208/787-2623, www.facebook.com, daily 4–11 P.M., $14–18), a busy spot with crunchy pizzas by the slice or pie, plus fresh beers from the on-the-premises brewery, darts, horseshoes, a pool table, and an outdoor beer garden.

DRIGGS

Driggs (pop. 1,500) is an odd conglomeration, mixing an old-time farming settlement and newfangled recreation mecca. It's also fast becoming a bedroom community for commuters to Jackson Hole. A major development on the south end of town brought many more homes and businesses, and the airport keeps expanding with giant hangars for all those private jets. There isn't much to downtown Driggs, so it's pretty easy to find your way around. After a decade of rapid growth, things have slowed in the last few years—much to the relief of some locals who feared another Jackson Hole scenario.

Sights

New in 2011, the **Greater Yellowstone Regional Geotourism Center** (60 S. Main St., www.yellowstonegeotourism.org, daily in summer, reduced winter hours) provides an outstanding introduction to the region. Historical

© DON PITCHER

the Spud Drive-In, Driggs

exhibits cover the original Native American inhabitants, mountain men, emigrants, Mormon settlers, and the rise of agriculture. Other exhibits focus on scenic byways and a National Geographic display on geotourism around Yellowstone. Especially notable are 24 prints and reproductions of Yellowstone paintings by Thomas Moran and historical photos by William Henry Jackson. One of these is a beautiful reproduction of *The Three Tetons;* the original hangs in the Oval Office of the White House. Also inside the center is a gift shop and visitor information kiosk.

Find local information at **Teton Valley Chamber of Commerce** (255 S. Main St., 208/354-2500, www.tetonvalleychamber. com, 10 A.M.–3 P.M. Mon.–Fri.) in downtown Driggs.

A mile south of Driggs is the delightfully amusing **Spud Drive-In** (208/354-2727 or 800/799-7783, www.spuddrivein.com), here since 1953 but now with a Dolby sound system. You can't miss the big truck out front with a flatbed-size "potato" on the back. The drive-in even attracts folks from Jackson, who cross the pass for an evening of fun beneath the stars. The drive-in is locally famous for Gladys burgers and Spud buds—served by carhops. The Spud also serves as a venue for summer concerts.

Spacious **Teton Valley Museum** (137 N. Hwy. 33, 208/354-6000, 10 A.M.–5 P.M. Tues.–Sat. late May–Oct., $5 adults, $2 kids, $15 families) houses historical displays from the valley's past on two floors, with a separate building containing old farm equipment. It's on the north side of town just beyond the Super 8 Motel.

At the airport just north of town, **Warbirds Museum** houses an interesting collection of restored historic planes in a hangar at the Teton Aviation Center (208/354-3100 or 800/472-6382, www.tetonaviation.com, free). Access is through the adjacent Warbirds Café. The collection contains several unusual fighter aircraft—including a T-28 Trojan and a Mig 15—but only four are displayed at any given time.

Shopping

Yöstmark Mountain Equipment (285 E. Little Ave., 208/354-2828, www.yostmark. com) sells a wide range of outdoor equipment. They also rent cross-country skis, skate skis, snowboards, telemark and alpine touring skis, and guide backcountry ski tours in winter.

Browse the eclectic selection of regional books at friendly **Dark Horse Books** (76 N. Main St., 208/354-8882 or 888/424-8882). Adjacent to the airport, the **Community Art Center** (8 Rodeo Dr., 208/354-4278, www. tetonartscouncil.com) exhibits works by regional artists.

A few miles north of Driggs, **Drawknife Billiards** (5146 N. Hwy. 33, 800/320-0527, www.drawknife.com) creates one-of-a-kind pool tables using hand-carved lodgepole bases and top-quality tabletops.

Accommodations

Just a block from the center of town is a delightful European-style guesthouse built in 1900, **The Pines Motel Guest Haus** (105 S. Main St., www.thepinestetonvalley.com, 208/354-2774 or 800/354-2778). The Neilson family provides seven rooms with private baths, each different but all nicely appointed with tasteful touches such as handmade quilts, along with Wi-Fi and an outdoor hot tub. Rates are very reasonable ($55–65 d or $110 for a two-room suite that sleeps eight) and kids are welcome.

On the north side of Driggs, **Super 8 Motel** (133 Hwy. 33, 208/354-8888 or 800/800-8000, www.super8.com) has standard rooms ($88 d) and suites that sleep four ($150). Amenities include an indoor pool, sauna, hot tub, Wi-Fi, and continental breakfast.

On the north side of Driggs, **Best Western Teton West** (476 N. Main St., 208/354-2363 or 800/528-1234, www.bestwestern.com, $120–130 d) features a light breakfast, indoor pool, hot tub, and Wi-Fi. Closed mid-October–mid-November.

Located a mile east of town, **Teton Valley Cabins** (34 E. Ski Hill Rd., 208/354-8153 or 866/687-1522, www.tetonvalleycabins.com,

$79–99 d) rents comfortable, modern duplex cabins. Most have kitchenettes, and families appreciate units with bunk beds. A hot tub is available, along with Wi-Fi.

Short-term bookings for town houses, homes, cabins, and condos in the area are provided by **Grand Valley Lodging** (208/354-8890 or 800/746-5518, www.grandvalleylodging.com). Rates range $80–500 per night, higher around Christmas and the Fourth of July. These accommodations are popular with families and groups heading to Grand Targhee Ski Resort.

Camping

The nearest public campsites are at **Teton Canyon Campground** (reserve at 518/885-3639 or 877/444-6777, www.recreation.gov, $9 fee, late May–mid-Sept., $10 per site), 11 miles east of Driggs in the Tetons. This is a delightful camping spot, and the trailhead into beautiful (and very popular) Alaska Basin is nearby.

Food

One benefit of Teton Valley's growth is a dramatic improvement in the local restaurant scene. Driggs now has several excellent dining places.

Teton Thai (18 N. Main St., 208/787-8424, www.tetonthai.com, daily 11:30 A.M.–2:30 P.M., 5:30–9:30 P.M.), a Jackson Hole favorite, has expanded and offers the same menu of South Asian favorites—including noodle, rice, and curry dishes—in a busy downtown Driggs setting. Most entrées are $12–14, but lighter options such as satay chicken or tom kha gai soup are about $8.

After a spicy Thai dinner, nothing hits the spot like something cold. Head a few doors up the street to **Teton Valley Creamery** (20 N. Main St., 208/354-0404, noon–9 P.M. Tues.–Sun. in summer, 2–9 P.M. Thurs.–Sun. in winter) for a gelato ($2.50). Made on the premises from local milk, gelato flavors include huckleberry, raspberry, and dulce de leche, plus the standard chocolate and vanilla. The owners also produce a variety of raw-milk artisanal cheeses.

Tiny **Wrap and Roll** (65 S. Main St., 208/354-7655, www.facebook.com, 11 A.M.–4 P.M. Mon.–Fri., $6–8) is a good lunch spot, with Greek chicken wraps, shrimp spring rolls, rice bowls, and more. Get it to go or take a seat at the picnic table out front.

On the north end of town across from the airport, **Hacienda Ccuajimalpa** (528 Valley Centre Dr., 208/354-0121, daily 10 A.M.–10 P.M., $4–8) serves inexpensive and authentic Mexican meals: chile rellenos, chimichangas, enchiladas, quesadillas, tamales, burritos, and tostadas.

Best place for an organic latte, fruit smoothie, or gourmet hot chocolate? Head over to **Cocoa Grove** (180 S. Main St., 208/354-2899, www.facebook.com, 6 A.M.–7 P.M. Mon.–Sat., 8 A.M.–5 P.M. Sun.); it's in the mall with Broulim's. The owners hail from Seattle, and really know coffee.

You won't find burgers or steaks at **Miso Hungry Café** (165 N. Main St., 208/354-8015, www.facebook.com, 11 A.M.–3 P.M. Mon.–Sat., 5:30–9 P.M. Mon.–Tues. and Thurs.–Fri., $14–20), a playful spot with covered tables on the front porch and a flavorful globe-trotting fare. The lunch menu includes Thai noodle bowl, Greek Athenian plate, Philly cheese steaks, and a variety of soups, salads, homemade breads, espresso, and desserts. Even the potato chips are made on the premises from local (of course) Idaho potatoes. Dinner features paella, chicken sorrentino, rack of lamb, and curried shrimp. Check the chalkboard for daily specials.

An aviation-themed restaurant at—appropriately enough—Driggs Airport just north of town, **Warbirds Café** (208/354-2550, www.tetonaviation.com, 11 A.M.–2 P.M. Mon.–Fri., 5–9 P.M. Tues.–Sat., $15–28) has windows facing the taxiway, and several tables on the patio provide an even closer view. The dinner menu includes such treats as bacon-wrapped beef tenderloin, buffalo burgers, and big Caesar salads. Several restored old planes fill the adjacent hangar. Warbirds Café is popular with pilots, who can fly in for lunch with a view and an upscale meal. Or, as one local pointed out,

© DON PITCHER

Warbirds Museum

it represents "all the things we ran away from when we moved here from Jackson." Dinner reservations are recommended.

Find Martha Pendl's amazing Austrian pastries and other treats at **(Pendal's Bakery & Café** (40 Depot St., 208/354-5623, www.pendlspastries.com, 7 A.M.–4 P.M. Mon.–Fri., 7 A.M.–3 P.M. Sat., 8 A.M.–3 P.M. Sun.). Ignore the official address; it's actually at the back of the public parking lot on Bates Road (and almost directly behind the bookstore). Get a coffee and one of the incredibly delectable treats: Nussknacker, Linzertorte, or Florentiner pastries. Lunchtime soups, sandwiches, and quiches follow. Pendl's is occasionally open for dinner in the summer.

Get malts, shakes, and hot fudge sundaes at the old-fashioned soda fountain inside **Corner Drug** (10 S. Main St., 208/354-2334, www.facebook.com, 9 A.M.–6:30 P.M. Mon.–Sat.). Lime freezes and huckleberry shakes ($4) are their claim to fame.

For late-night foraging and all-around wonderful meals, head to **(Forage Bistro & Lounge** (385 Little Ave., 208/354-2858, www.forageandlounge.com, 4–10 P.M. Tues.–Sun.,

$10–22) a few blocks east of downtown. This trendy and very hip spot has a brick-paved deck out front and a curvy bar inside with a handful of tables. The limited, moderately priced menu changes seasonally, but typically includes noodles with coconut, garlic, ginger, and peanuts, a cheeseburger with chive aioli, red pepper, onion, and potato wedges, halibut with rice noodle salad, and an "everything" salad.

Shop for groceries at **Broulim's** (52 S. Main St., 208/354-2350, www.broulims.com, 7 A.M.–11 P.M. Mon.–Sat.). There's also a sushi bar, deli, and pizza by the slice. Just up the street is **Barrels and Bins Community Market** (36 S. Main St., 208/354-2307, daily 9 A.M.–7 P.M.), selling health foods, organic produce, and other earthy fare. The **Teton Valley Open Air Market** (208/351-4317, mid-June–Sept.) comes to downtown Driggs Fridays 9 A.M.–2 P.M., with produce, crafts, flowers, and baked goods.

Services

Get Caribou-Targhee National Forest information from the **Teton Basin Ranger District Office** (just south of town at 525 S. Main St.,

208/354-2312, www.fs.fed.us/r4/caribou-targhee).

Wash clothes at **Extra Sock Laundry,** next to Subway on the north end of town.

Teton Valley Hospital (120 E. Howard Ave., 208/354-2383, www.tetonvalleyhospital.com) is available for emergencies.

Rent cars from **Basin Auto Rental** (180 N. Main St., 208/354-2297, www.basinautorental.com).

Catch a ride with **Teton Valley Taxi** (208/313-2728).

START Buses (307/733-4521, www.startbus.com, $8 one-way) provide year-round weekday service connecting Driggs and Victor with Jackson.

TETONIA

Eight miles north of Driggs, sleepy Tetonia is dominated by a big LDS church, with dirt side streets. Potato farms and grand old barns spread across the surrounding landscape; it's a good place to see kids riding horseback. The crest of the tourist wave is just starting to lap at the shores of Tetonia, and at last check no local place sold espresso, focaccia, or cell phones.

Three miles south of Tetonia, **Blue Fly Gallery** (208/456-0900, www.kenmorrisonfineart.com) exhibits the colorful paintings and sculptures of Ken Morrison.

Steve Horn Mountain Gallery (112 S. Main St., 208/456-2719, www.stevehorn.com) crafts rugged Old West-style furniture and relief carvings.

Accommodations and Food

Teton Mountain View Lodge & RV Park (208/456-2741, www.tetonmountainlodge.com) has comfortable motel rooms ($79–89 d) with Wi-Fi, continental breakfast, and hot tub access. RV spaces are $29, and tent sites cost $10.

North End Bar & Grill (208/456-2202, daily 7 A.M.–10 P.M. in summer, 8 A.M.–9 P.M. in winter, $10–25) attracts local farmers (and travelers) with filling biscuits-and-gravy breakfasts (along with some lighter fare), lunchtime buffalo burgers, Cajun chicken sandwiches, and fish tacos, plus dinners that include blackened halibut, rib-eye steak, and weekend prime rib.

GRAND TARGHEE SKI RESORT

On the west side of the Tetons 42 miles from Jackson, Grand Targhee Ski Resort (in Alta, 307/353-2300 or 800/827-4433, www.grandtarghee.com) offers the friendliness of a small resort with the amenities and snow you'd expect at a major one. To get here you'll need to drive into Idaho and turn east at Driggs. The resort sits at the end of a beautiful road 12 miles east of Driggs and just six miles inside Wyoming. Its motto says it all: "Snow from heaven, not from hoses." With an annual snowfall topping 500 inches (42 feet!)—most of which is champagne powder—Targhee became the spot where powderhounds got all they could ever want. Ski magazines consistently rank it as having North America's best (or second-best) snow. In fact, the resort guarantees its snow: If you find conditions not to your liking, you can turn in your ticket within an hour of purchase and get a "snow check" good for another day of skiing. By the way, the official name is Grand Targhee Ski and Summer Resort, but most folks call it Grand Targhee, or simply Targhee.

The biggest drawback to Grand Targhee Ski Resort is the same thing that makes it so great—the weather. Lots of snow means lots of clouds and storms, and because it snows so much there are many days when the name cynics apply—"Grand Foghee"—seems more appropriate. Many folks who have returned to Targhee year after year have still not seen the magnificent Grand Teton backdrop behind the ski area! Be sure to bring your goggles. The quad lift up Peaked Mountain provides intermediate skiing on slopes that are more protected and suffer less wind and fog.

Skiing and Snowboarding

The resort has two quads, one double chairlift, and a surface lift on Fred's Mountain, plus a quad on adjacent Peaked Mountain. The top elevation is 10,230 feet, with the longest run dropping 2,822 feet over almost three miles. About 750 acres are groomed, but you'll always find track-free skiing on the remaining 2,250 acres of ungroomed powder, so bring your snorkel. In addition, snowcat skiing ($349 per day including lunch) is offered on a 1,000-acre section of Peaked Mountain reserved for powderhounds.

Lift tickets at Grand Targhee cost $69 per day ($49 half-day) for adults and $29 per day for children ages 6–14 and seniors (free under age six). Substantial discounts are offered for multi-day lift tickets or lodging-and-ski packages.

Fully 70 percent of Targhee's groomed runs are intermediate to advanced-intermediate, but advanced skiers will find an extraordinary number of deep-powder faces to explore. The ski school offers lessons for all abilities, and children's programs make it possible for parents to leave their kids behind. Cross-country skiers enjoy the Nordic center, and ski and snowboard rentals are available at the base of the mountain. The ski area usually opens in mid-November and closes in mid-April, although some years you may be able to ski even into July. Lifts operate daily 9 A.M.–4 P.M.

Winter Activities

Teton Ice Park (307/690-1385 or 888/864-8029, www.tetonice.com) is a 40-foot ice waterfall where you can learn climbing techniques. Half-day guided climbs (with all gear) are $225 for one person or $300 for two.

Excellent guided **snowshoe wildlife tours** (free if you have snowshoes, $10 to rent them) will appeal to amateur naturalists, and on the **sleigh-ride dinner** ($40 adults, $15 kids), you'll ride in a horse-drawn sleigh to a yurt where a Western-style meal is served. Targhee's **tubing park** (opens at 5 P.M.; $10) is a fun place for kids to slide down a snowy hill. A **Kid's Club** at Targhee provides supervised child care for children under six, and teens can join special programs that include skiing and other fun on the mountain.

Summer Activities

Not far from Grand Targhee are several popular summertime hiking trails within the Jedediah Smith Wilderness.

The resort is a popular place to relax in the summer and offers many activities. A quad chairlift ($15 adults, $6 kids) takes you up the 10,200-foot summit of Fred's Mountain for strikingly close views of the Tetons. The lift operates daily late June–mid-September. A Forest Service naturalist leads guided walks twice daily.

Horseback rides and lessons are a favorite Targhee summertime activity; one-hour rides are $39. The area is also a fun mountain-biking destination, with bike rentals; you can also take them up the chairlift ($20). The big climbing wall ($10 for an introductory climb) is open to all abilities and is a good place to learn some basic—or advanced—moves. Other summer activities and facilities at Targhee include basketball courts, an outdoor swimming pool and hot tubs, a fitness center, horseshoes, tennis, disc golf, archery, and volleyball. The nine-hole **Targhee Village Golf Course** (208/354-8577 or 307/353-8577, www.targheevillage.com) is just down the road. After all this excitement, you'll probably want to relax with a massage, aromatherapy, facial, or steam bath at the on-site spa.

Events

End the year—and start a new one—with **Torchlight Parades** at Grand Targhee on the evenings of December 25 and 31. Also on New Year's Eve is a fireworks display over the mountain. Each March, the resort celebrates telemark skiing with the **Targhee Tele Fest.** Ski races of all sorts take place, and Targhee rocks to great music, an outdoor barbecue, and fun events. Close out winter with mid-April's **Cardboard Box Derby,** where participants swoosh down the ski hill on bizarre cardboard creations.

The resort pulls out the stops for two very popular musical events: **Targhee Fest** in mid-July with a mix of nationally known rock and folk artists—from Michael Franti to Los Lobos—plus **Targhee Bluegrass Festival** in mid-August. Bring your dancin' shoes! The music attracts hundreds of people, so call the resort well ahead of time for camping or lodging reservations.

Accommodations

Three lodges at the base of the mountain— Targhee Lodge, Teewinot Lodge, and Sioux Lodge—offer ski-in, ski-out access, a large heated outdoor pool, a hot tub, and a workout room. Rates quoted are for the winter holiday season; they're approximately 40 percent lower in summer. Contact Targhee (307/353-2300 or 800/827-4433, www.grandtarghee.com) for details on lodging options at or near the resort. Most lodging places are closed October–mid-November and mid-April–mid-June.

Get standard motel accommodations at **Targhee Lodge** with holiday winter rates of $179–199 for up to four. Deluxe hotel rooms ($245–270 d) with lodgepole furnishings and access to an indoor hot tub are at **Teewinot Lodge.** The lobby here is a fine place to relax in front of the fire on winter evenings. **Sioux Lodge** continues the Western theme with lodgepole furnishings, and it also has kitchenettes, adobe-style fireplaces, and small balconies. Studio units are $289–319 for up to four people, loft units $359–395 for four people, and two-bedroom units run $495–545.

Off-site lodging (approximately 10 miles downhill from Grand Targhee) includes one-, two-, and three-bedroom condominiums and town houses. Nightly holiday-season rates start at $230 d for one-bedroom condos and go up to $485 for three-bedroom town houses. The minimum stay at all Targhee-managed lodging places is two nights most of the year, or five nights during peak winter periods.

You can cut these lodging rates by avoiding the Christmas–New Year's and Spring Break rush periods. More substantial discounts are available if you ski or snowboard during the value season before mid-December or after late March.

Ski packages are a fine bargain, starting around $188 per day at Targhee Lodge (unavailable Dec. 25–Jan. 1). Packages include lodging and lift tickets for two adults and two kids under age 13, plus two free ski lessons. Summer lodging is surprisingly reasonable, with such options as rafting trips, scenic chairlift, and spa amenities.

Food

At the base of Grand Targhee is a compact cluster of shops. You won't have to walk far to find a cafeteria, pizza place, sandwich shop, burger joint, and general store. The nicest place is **Branding Iron Grill** (7:30 A.M.–9 P.M. daily in summer) serving hearty breakfasts and lunches, along with cozy dinners. Grand Targhee's social center is the **Trap Bar** (Thurs.–Sat. 11 A.M.– 8:30 P.M., Sun. 11 A.M.–5 P.M. in summer) featuring live music all winter (Thurs.–Sat.), sporting events on the flat-screen TVs, and pub grub on the menu all the time. Guests at Targhee can also take a **horse-drawn sleigh** on a 15-minute ride to a Mongolian-style yurt for a home-cooked steak or chicken dinner. The price is $40 ($15 for kids ages 5–12), and reservations are required. Other shops here sell groceries, ski and snowboard gear, clothing, and gifts.

Getting There and Around

Grand Targhee is 42 miles northwest of Jackson on the western side of the Tetons in Alta, Wyoming. Get there by driving over Teton Pass (occasionally closed by winter storms), north through Victor and Driggs, Idaho, and then east back into Wyoming.

The **Targhee Express/Alltrans** bus makes daily wintertime trips (90 minutes each way) to Grand Targhee from Jackson Hole. Buses pick up skiers from Jackson and Teton Village hotels shortly after 7 A.M., returning from Targhee at 4:30 P.M. for a round-trip fare of $88, including a full-day lift ticket. Round-trip bus fare without a lift ticket costs $44. Reservations are required; make them before 9 P.M. on the night before by calling 307/733-3135 or 800/443-6133, or book online at www. jacksonholealltrans.com. Van service is also available year-round to airports in Jackson, Salt Lake City, and Idaho Falls.

www.moon.com

DESTINATIONS | ACTIVITIES | BLOGS | MAPS | BOOKS

MOON.COM is ready to help plan your next trip! Filled with fresh trip ideas and strategies, author interviews, informative travel blogs, a detailed map library, and descriptions of all the Moon guidebooks, Moon.com is all you need to get out and explore the world—or even places in your own backyard. While at Moon.com, sign up for our monthly e-newsletter for updates on new releases, travel tips, and expert advice from our on-the-go Moon authors. As always, when you travel with Moon, expect an experience that is uncommon and truly unique.

MAP SYMBOLS

▬▬▬ Expressway	⬛ Highlight	✗ Airfield	⚓ Golf Course
▬▬▬ Primary Road	○ City/Town	✈ Airport	🅿 Parking Area
▬▬▬ Secondary Road	◉ State Capital	▲ Mountain	⬟ Archaeological Site
═ ═ ═ Unpaved Road	⊛ National Capital	✛ Unique Natural Feature	⛪ Church
- - - - Trail	★ Point of Interest		
·········· Ferry	• Accommodation	⚐ Waterfall	⛽ Gas Station
▬▬▬ Railroad	▼ Restaurant/Bar	▲ Park	◌ Glacier
▬▬▬ Pedestrian Walkway	■ Other Location	ⓘ Trailhead	Mangrove
▥ Stairs	Λ Campground	🎿 Skiing Area	Reef
			Swamp

CONVERSION TABLES

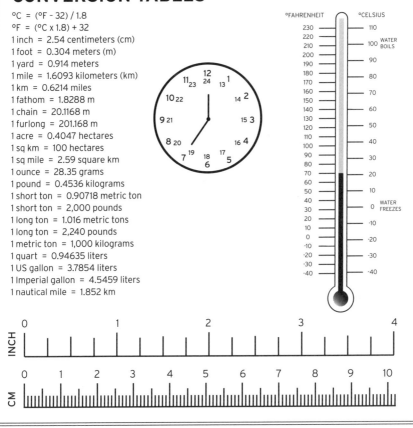

$$°C = (°F - 32) / 1.8$$
$$°F = (°C \times 1.8) + 32$$

1 inch = 2.54 centimeters (cm)
1 foot = 0.304 meters (m)
1 yard = 0.914 meters
1 mile = 1.6093 kilometers (km)
1 km = 0.6214 miles
1 fathom = 1.8288 m
1 chain = 20.1168 m
1 furlong = 201.168 m
1 acre = 0.4047 hectares
1 sq km = 100 hectares
1 sq mile = 2.59 square km
1 ounce = 28.35 grams
1 pound = 0.4536 kilograms
1 short ton = 0.90718 metric ton
1 short ton = 2,000 pounds
1 long ton = 1.016 metric tons
1 long ton = 2,240 pounds
1 metric ton = 1,000 kilograms
1 quart = 0.94635 liters
1 US gallon = 3.7854 liters
1 Imperial gallon = 4.5459 liters
1 nautical mile = 1.852 km

MOON SPOTLIGHT JACKSON HOLE, WYOMING

Avalon Travel
a member of the Perseus Books Group
1700 Fourth Street
Berkeley, CA 94710, USA
www.moon.com

Editor and Series Manager: Sabrina Young
Copy Editor: Lisa Wolff
Production and Graphics Coordinator:
  Lucie Ericksen
Cover Designer: Kathryn Osgood
Map Editor: Brice Ticen
Cartographers: Kat Bennett, Andrea Butkovic,
  Chris Henrick

ISBN-13: 978-1-59880-922-0

Text © 2011 by Don Pitcher.
Maps © 2011 by Avalon Travel.
All rights reserved.

Some photos and illustrations are used by permission and are the property of the original copyright owners.

Front cover photo: © Don Pitcher
Title page photo: © Don Pitcher

Printed in Canada by Friesens

ABOUT THE AUTHOR

Don Pitcher

Perhaps Don Pitcher's love of travel came about because he moved so much as a child; by age 15 he had lived in six states and two dozen East Coast and Midwestern towns. Don's family hails from Maine, but he was born in Atlanta, making him a southerner with New England blood. He moved west for college, receiving a master's degree from the University of California, Berkeley, where his thesis examined wildfires in the high elevation forests of Sequoia National Park. When his first (and only) scientific paper was published, he appeared headed into the world of ecological research.

Don then landed what seemed the coolest job on the planet shortly after grad school: being flown around Alaska's massive Wrangell-St. Elias National Park in a helicopter while conducting fire research. Wild places continued to beckon, and over the next 15 years Don built backcountry trails, worked as a wilderness ranger, mapped grizzly habitat, and operated salmon weirs — anything to avoid an office job. After that first season in Alaska, he spent three months in the South Pacific, and quickly found himself addicted to travel. His explorations eventually took him to 35 countries and all 50 states.

After authoring his first book, *Berkeley Inside/Out*, Don went on to write *Moon Yellowstone & Grand Teton, Moon Alaska, Moon Wyoming*, and *Moon San Juan Islands*. He has produced three photographic books, served as editor for Best Places Alaska, and is a contributor to Triporati.com and other websites. Don's photos have appeared in a multitude of publications and advertisements, and his prints are sold in many Alaska and Washington galleries. He is also a highly regarded wedding photographer.

Don lives in Homer, Alaska with his wife, Karen Shemet, and their children, Aziza and Rio. Get details on his latest writing and photography projects — along with links to many of the places mentioned in this book — at www.DonPitcher.com, or find him on Facebook.